p.55

* difference b/w
women + work.
college educ (w child)
non-college educ (w child)
what factors?
- family?
- husband?
- short?

p 59 quote?
Achievemt

(p 62) quote

D0874093

WOMEN IN TRANSITION

CAREER, FAMILY, AND LIFE SATISFACTION IN THREE COHORTS

BY
CATHERINE A. FAVER

PRAEGER

PRAEGER SPECIAL STUDIES • PRAEGER SCIENTIFIC

New York • Philadelphia • Eastbourne, UK
Toronto • Hong Kong • Tokyo • Sydney

Library of Congress Cataloging in Publication Data

Faver, Catherine A.
    Women in transition.

    Bibliography: p.
    Includes index.
    1. Women—United States—Attitudes. 2. Women—Employ-
ment—United States. 3. Achievement motivation.
4. Family—United States. 5. Contentment. 6. Life cycle,
Human. I. Title.
HQ1420.F34   1984   305.4   84-8246
ISBN 0-03-072026-5 (alk. paper)

Pages 29-32, 39-41, 73-76, 99-102, 120-23, 137-39. Portions of these pages were
excerpted or adapted from Catherine A. Faver, "Women, Careers, and Family:
Generational and Life-Cycle Effects on Achievement Orientation," *Journal of
Family Issues* 2 (March 1981):91-112. Copyright 1981 by Sage Publications, Inc.
Used by permission.

Pages 43-47. Portions of this section were excerpted or adapted from Catherine
A. Faver, "Achievement Orientation, Attainment Values, and Women's Employment," *Journal of Vocational Behavior* 20 (February 1982):67-80. Copyright
1982 by Academic Press, Inc. Used by permission.

Pages 70-71, 83-84, 140-42, 145-48. From Mary Frank Fox and Sharlene Hesse-
Biber, *Women at Work* (Palo Alto, Ca.: Mayfield Publishing Company, 1984).
Reprinted by permission.

Published in 1984 by Praeger Publishers
CBS Educational and Professional Publishing,
a Division of CBS Inc.
521 Fifth Avenue, New York, NY 10175 USA

Printed in the United States of America
on acid-free paper

ACKNOWLEDGMENTS

I am grateful to Jean Campbell, Hazel Markus, and Jean Manis of the University of Michigan Center for Continuing Education of Women for making available the data for this project.

With his guidance and encouragement, Dr. Gayl Ness greatly facilitated the study.

Dr. Mary Frank Fox, who provided invaluable editorial assistance on the manuscript, is an inspiration to me in the quality of her scholarship, the strength of her commitment, and her unselfish support.

CONTENTS

LIST OF TABLES

1.

WOMEN, ACHIEVEMENT, AND LIFE SATISFACTION: THE WORK AND FAMILY CONTEXT

During recent decades, remarkable and far-reaching changes have occurred in women's participation in work and family roles. To begin with, women's labor force participation has increased dramatically since World War II, so that today, paid employment is part of the lives of most American women (see Fox & Hesse-Biber 1984: 1, 4; Hesselbart 1980). Furthermore, since about 1960, changes in women's family roles have become evident. More women are divorcing, and they are divorcing at earlier ages. At the same time, young women are delaying first marriage and motherhood, and many are deciding not to have children at all. Thus, in the course of social change, the "usual" life pattern of women has been altered substantially (see Huston-Stein & Higgins-Trenk 1978).

Despite these important changes, there are equally important areas of continuity in women's lives. Regardless of their employment status, most women retain primary household and child-care responsibilities. Moreover, the institutional structures of the economy and the labor force are still built on the assumption of the traditional nuclear family, which includes one full-time worker and one full-time homemaker (see Fox & Hesse-Biber 1984: 179, 196).

These areas of social change and stability are mirrored in the lives of individual women as they move in and out of family and employment roles. While behavioral patterns and trends are fairly easy to document with survey and census data, much less is known about areas of stability and change, continuity and discontinuity in women's attitudes toward family and employment. What is the relationship between social change, social roles, and individual values and attitudes? As women experience transitions in their work and family roles, to what extent do their attitudes and values also change? Are women's aspirations and values consistent with their work and family roles, or are there discrepancies between values and roles? Are the discrepancies between values and roles greater for some groups of women than for others? Are they greater, for example, among women of certain ages or life-cycle stages? How do these discrepancies between women's values and roles affect their general well-being?

This book addresses these questions as it reports a study of women's career and family attitudes in the context of social change. In addressing these issues, the study has a unifying theme, a specific focus, and a distinct perspective. The theme of the study is transition: individual transitions from one life-cycle stage to the next, and societal transition from one generation to the next. The specific focus is the expression of women's achievement orientation through career and family, and the relationship of values and roles to overall life satisfaction. The perspective is social psychological, considering both social roles and individual values as they affect the context and quality of life at each age and life-cycle stage.

ADULT DEVELOPMENT: CONCEPTS AND ISSUES

Research on changes occurring during adulthood are part of the study of adult development, a relatively new, interdisciplinary field for social scientists. Thus far, most of the empirical studies of adult development have focused on men's lives, and have drawn their samples from the group of individuals born during the depression of the 1930s (Rossi 1980). In the growing literature on adult development, various theoretical perspectives are emerging, and several social scientists have constructed typologies by which to characterize and classify these perspectives (see, e.g., Brim 1976; Rossi 1980; Troll 1975). Brim (1976), for example, characterizes the perspectives according to whether the study of personality change emphasizes internal, intrapsychic events or external changes, such as changes in social status (Rossi 1980).

From its initial concern primarily with age-correlated changes in personality, the study of adult development has broadened to include the effects of sociocultural and historical changes on individual development (Huston-Stein & Higgins-Trenk 1978; Baltes, Cornelius & Nesselroade 1977). The present study similarly adopts a broad view of adult development. With a social psychological perspective, we consider the effects of historical changes, differences in social roles, and variations in life-course patterns on both the attitudes and the behavior patterns of women in various age groups and life-cycle stages. Moreover, we examine the interactive effects of individual values and social roles on women's well-being.

In the study of adult development, we use several key concepts and terms: age cohort, generation, life cycle, and life course. "Age cohort" can be defined as "a group of people who have been born at the same time and who have therefore grown up under the same historical circumstances" (Troll 1975:10). Thus, an age or birth cohort is essentially an age group; it consists of people who were born between some specified dates or within certain time limits (Troll 1975). Because they grew up under particular historical circumstances, an age cohort "will be different in many ways from people who grew up at a different time" (Troll 1975:10). Each age cohort may be thought of as "representing a past 'culture' level--or . . . 'world'--that obtained during its early years of socialization" (Bernard 1981:127). Practically speaking, "One's world is different according to when one is born, when one grows up, when one marries, bears children, loses a husband, or becomes widowed" (Bernard 1981:126).

Closely related to the concept of cohort is that of generation. According to Bernard (1981:126), French and German sociologists developed the concept of a political or social generation "to refer to people subjected to common historical events which they share because of when they were born." Indeed, "Wars, depressions, strikes, reforms, crises of many kinds leave indelible imprints on those growing up when these events happen" (Bernard 1981:126). When such major historical events separate cohorts, they mark generations. Thus, generational differences result from the discontinuities created by the differential impact of historical events on age cohorts (Berger 1960; Zeitlin 1967). In general, this suggests that we may expect women in different age cohorts in our sample to differ in certain attitudes and behavior patterns.

But the women in our sample may also vary in attitudes and behaviors because they are in different stages in the life cycle. In general, the concept of the life cycle, as studied by sociologists, "emphasizes the major changes in social roles which succeed each other during the adult years" (Campbell 1981:182). The concept of life cycle has commonly been applied to both individuals and families. Recently, however, some social scientists studying individual development have adopted slightly different terms, or conceptual labels, for their study of the human life cycle. Many sociologists tend to use the term "life course," while psychologists use the term "life span" as they take different perspectives and focus on different variables (Rossi 1980:7).

Although the concept of life cycle is quite old, there has been great variation historically in the definitions and labels of its stages (Bernard 1975). In the literature on the developmental approach to the study of the family, for example, a number of different ways of defining family life-cycle stages have been suggested (see, e.g., Cavan 1974; Hill & Rodgers 1964). Among the various classification schemes proposed to describe the individual life cycle or life course, Campbell's (1981) list of stages is particularly useful. He specifies "six major stages through which most people pass and several noncomforming situations in which smaller numbers of people find themselves at some time during their lives" (Campbell 1981:182). The six major stages are early unmarried adulthood; early childless marriage; married with preschool child; married with school-age children; married with youngest child over 17; and widowhood. The four situations that relatively fewer people experience are over 30 years old, never married; over 30 years old, married with no children; separated or divorced; and unmarried parent (Campbell 1981:182-83).

Characterizing or defining the life-cycle stages of women requires some special considerations. Traditionally, women's primary social roles have been the family roles of wife and mother. Because of the recent large-scale entrance of women, especially married mothers, into the labor force, however, a thorough understanding of women's life cycle requires consideration of both family and worker roles (Bernard 1975). Recent research has thus focused on the ways women combine these roles across the life span (Bernard 1971). As Taeuber and Sweet (1976) note, however, paid employment for women is not tied as closely to any age period as are such family-related events as marriage and childbearing and child rearing. Thus, age, family roles, or a combination of these variables seems most useful for defining women's life-cycle stages.

Bernard (1975) offers a parsimonious way of focusing on both the individual life course and the family roles of women by dividing the adult female life cycle into three stages: early motherhood, during which there is at least one pre-school child in the home; middle motherhood, when the youngest child is in elementary or secondary school; and late motherhood, or the period often referred to as the "empty nest" stage, when the children have completed high school and have been launched from the home.

Bernard's (1975) specification of these three general stages of motherhood, along with the stages in the individual life cycle outlined by Campbell (1981) and listed above, form the conceptual framework for the family life-cycle stages and individual life-course patterns that we will be examining among the women in our study. In Chapter 2 we will describe our operational definitions of these basic concepts.

Because age is a critical variable in the study of adult development, it is necessary at this point to discuss the concept of age, particularly as it relates to our study of generational and life-cycle transitions in women's lives. As Elder (1975:165) notes, age or birth year may be used as an indicator of three different variables:

> (a) the individual life time or life span from birth to death--chronological . . . age as an approximate index of stage in the aging process; (b) the social timetable of the life course (e.g., entry into marriage, retirement) . . . defined by age criteria in norms and social roles; and (c) historical time in the course of social change . . . .

According to this schema, age is an exact indicator of birth or age cohort (c), and thus locates one in history. But age is only an approximate indicator of developmental age, or stage in the aging process (a), and of one's probable social roles (b).

The multiple meanings of age are also implicit in Neugarten's (1977:34) discussion of time and the life course:

> ... time is at least a three-dimensional pheno- menon in charting the course of the life cycle, with historical time, life time (or chronological age) and social time all intricately intertwined.

Thus, the meaning of age has traditionally been "so- cially defined," in the sense that society has certain expec- tations regarding the appropriate behaviors for specific ages:

> Every society is age-graded, and every society has a system of social expectations regarding age- appropriate behavior. ... There exists a socially prescribed timetable for the ordering of major life events. ... Men and women are aware not only of the social clocks ... but also of their own timing; ... they readily describe themselves as "early," "late," or "on time" with regard to the major life events (Neugarten 1977:34).

Neugarten (1977:35) notes further that the timing and rhythm of the life cycle change with historical time, resulting in changes in societal age norms. In other words, the typical life-course pattern changes over time. In the study of adult development, this perspective focusing on the importance of societal age norms is part of the "timing-of-events" model (Rossi 1980).

Recently, however, theorists of adult development have noted a relaxation of age norms, so that there is a more "fluid life cycle, one marked by an increasing number of role transitions, the disappearance of traditional time- tables ... and the lack of synchrony among age-related roles" (Neugarten 1979:889, cited in Rossi 1980:16-17). Rossi (1980:16) elaborates on these recent changes in life course patterns:

> Many indicators in the late 1970s suggest a new
> period of increased variance in both the timing
> and sequencing of life events. Age norms are
> more fluid; more people marry, divorce, remarry,
> or never marry; . . . more people have no children
> at all, and more have late first births.

In light of the decreasing importance of age norms, and the
increasing numbers of role transitions that people experience,
age is likely to be less reliable as an indicator of an
individual's probable social roles than ever before.

As this brief discussion suggests, the use of age as a
variable in the study of adult development raises some
complex issues of data interpretation, particularly when
cross-sectional data are utilized. While longitudinal research
involves comparing the responses of the same group of
subjects at two or more points in time, cross-sectional
research involves comparing the responses of people of
different age groups at the same point in time. Thus, while
longitudinal research actually yields age changes, cross-
sectional research yields age differences (Schaie 1970, cited
in Troll 1975:9-10). Since we cannot assume that "age
difference equals age change" (Troll 1975:9), a number of
different interpretations may be given for observed differences in attitudes and behaviors of people of different
ages.

The present study uses cross-sectional data. Thus,
while we will be examining attitude and behavior differences
among women who vary in age, marital status, and parental
status, we are unable to examine changes that may occur as
women of different cohorts move through their individual life
courses. Nevertheless, we will be making some tentative
inferences regarding the nature and source of observed
differences among the women in our sample. At this point, it
may be useful to enumerate briefly the various causes, or
sources, of differences in attitudes, values, and behaviors
that may be observed among women of different ages.

First, differences among women of different ages may
be due to the physiological and biological effects of aging
(see Rossi 1980). Second, in cross-sectional analysis of data,
differences in age cohorts may result from "historical
changes in the socialization experiences of different cohorts"
or from the differential effects of current cultural changes

on adults of different ages (Huston-Stein & Higgins-Trenk 1978:260). These types of differences may thus reflect generational transitions. Third, differences among women of different ages may be due to differences in basic life-course pattern. In fact, even women of the same age may have different attitudes and values because they have adopted different social roles, as reflected in their marital, parental, and employment statuses. This raises the question of how adult development differs for women who follow the typical family life-cycle pattern of marriage and motherhood, compared with those who follow atypical, but increasingly common, life-course patterns, such as never marrying or remaining childless.

Fourth, attitudinal and behavioral differences among women of different ages may be related to differences in life-cycle stage. For example, even among women who follow the typical family life-cycle pattern, changes in attitudes, values, and behavior may occur as they move from one stage of the family life cycle to the next. Thus, some attitudinal and behavioral differences among women of different ages, or even of the same age, may reflect life-cycle transitions. Finally, differences among women of different ages may be due to differences in the timing of particular life-course events, such as marriage and childbearing. Several theorists have observed that the same event is experienced differently, depending on when it occurs in the life course (see, e.g., Bardwick 1980; Levinson et al. 1978). Such differences in the subjective experience of an event at different points in the life course may be due partially to the physiological and biological effects of aging (see Rossi 1980), noted above. For example, early motherhood (Daniels & Weingarten 1982) and middle motherhood (Rossi 1980) are experienced differently by women of different ages. This raises the question of which attitudinal and behavioral differences among women of different ages, or even of the same age, are due to differences in the timing of life-course events.

These potential sources of attitudinal and behavioral differences among women are not mutually exclusive. Thus, for example, women's values may differ both because of generational differences and because of differences in life-cycle stage. In interpreting the findings from cross-sectional data, however, it is important to understand each of these potential explanations for observed differences in respondents' attitudes and behaviors.

Having introduced some essential concepts and considerations in the study of adult development, we can now turn to the specific focus of our study: women's achievement orientation, and its expression through career and family, across generations and life-cycle stages.

WOMEN AND ACHIEVEMENT ORIENTATION: THEORY AND RESEARCH

Women's traditional roles as wives and mothers have profound effects on the patterning of their lives, and provide the structure on which attitudes and behaviors are built. This study focuses on the intertwining of women's life roles with their achievement orientation and the way it is expressed, both in the family and in career activity, across the life cycle. We propose that women's achievement orientation is rooted in early experience and stable throughout adulthood. However, the area in which achievement orientation is expressed--its channeling into the home or paid employment--depends primarily on a woman's position in the social structure and the social climate of her time. Furthermore, her general satisfaction with life is partly dependent on the degree of fit between her personal achievement values and structural opportunities for their expression. Before considering these hypotheses further, we must understand the major developments in the study of achievement orientation.

In its early conceptualization, achievement motivation was regarded as a desire to meet standards of excellence in whatever situation such standards apply (McClelland et al. 1953). Thus, it was considered to be a general motive for competence in any achievement area. Following its introduction, the achievement motive became the focus of numerous studies using projective measures for its assessment. On the basis of these studies, Veroff (Veroff et al. 1975:172) suggests that achievement motivation was defined as "a disposition to find gratification in successful competition with standards of excellence through one's own efforts" (italics in the original).

Yet the early work on achievement motivation showed that its original conceptualization was neither accurate nor appropriate for females. Further work indicates that its inapplicability to female achievement may be a result of several inadequacies in the original concept and its measurement.

First, achievement motivation was originally considered to be a unidimensional concept. But more recent research suggests that it is multidimensional (Veroff et al. 1975). Veroff and his associates used the more general term "achievement orientation" to refer to the multidimensional achievement motivation concept, and they identified a number of components of achievement orientation, including personal efficacy, or positive confidence in personal ability (Veroff et al. 1975), and self-esteem about achievement (Veroff et al. 1971).

Second, there was some controversy regarding the measurement of achievement motivation in the early studies. Specifically, the validity of the projective test frequently used to measure achievement motivation was questioned. As a result, paper-and-pencil tests to measure achievement motivation were developed and utilized (Denmark, Tangri & McCandless 1978; Veroff et al. 1975).

Finally, the original achievement motivation concept was inadequate because it did not allow for variations in the expression of achievement need. More specifically, the original concept was defined as a general motive leading to direct achievement behavior. To understand the achievement behavior of women, however, it is necessary to consider variations in two aspects of the expression of achievement orientation: the area in which achievement needs are expressed and the mode of their expression. Each aspect requires further discussion.

The line of theory and research dealing with the area in which achievement needs are expressed is particularly pertinent to the present study. In contrast with a general achievement motive, later studies suggested that individuals are motivated to achieve in specific areas (Crandall et al. 1960; Crandall & Battle 1970), and that achievement motivation may predict performance only when the goal of the behavior is considered valuable to the individual (French & Lesser 1964). Thus, the concept of attainment values is useful for understanding achievement behavior. Attainment values are "the value(s) an individual attaches to performing well in a given achievement area" (Stein & Bailey 1976:242).

Recognition that achievement motivation may be expressed in different areas has had an important effect on the understanding of the concept of achievement motivation. Thus, in light of recent research and theory, "Achievement is defined in terms of excellence, and achievement motivation is generally assumed to mean a concern for attaining excellence, whatever the behavioral domain" (Denmark, Tangri & McCandless 1978:408).

The concept of attainment values is critical in distinguishing between the affiliation and achievement needs of women. With different lines of reasoning, both Crandall (1963) and Veroff (1969) suggested that females strive to achieve in order to gain social approval; that is, the underlying motive is affiliation rather than achievement (see also Denmark, Tangri & McCandless 1978). Stein and Bailey (1976) argue, however, that women often strive to achieve in the areas of affiliation and social skills, but that their actual motive in many cases is achievement, or meeting a standard of excellence. The bulk of the evidence, they suggest, indicates that women do indeed strive for excellence, but that they are most likely to express their achievement needs in activities defined by society as "appropriate" for females.

Research on children has reflected this tendency for girls to assign higher value to sex-role-appropriate task areas (Stein et al. 1971). And French and Lesser (1964) noted that women may be more motivated to achieve in women's traditional roles than in intellectual pursuits. More recently, Hoffman (1975) suggested that some women define affiliation as success; for example, marriage is an important achievement goal for many women. To summarize, affiliation may be an important achievement goal for many women; and achievement orientation, or striving to attain excellence, can be expressed in the areas of affiliation and social skills.

The channeling of women's achievement strivings into tasks and areas that are considered to be "sex-role-appropriate" is understandable in light of the negative sanctions that have frequently been applied to women who deviate from traditional roles. Horner's (1972) research on the motive to avoid success was based on the assumption that women associate success in intellectual endeavors with social rejection. Reassessments of this research, however, suggested that "avoidance of success" was not a motive but, rather, a realistic attitude reflecting knowledge of the consequences of deviation from sex-role prescriptions (Condry & Dyer 1976).

In addition to the fear of social rejection, women's achievement orientation is powerfully channeled into traditionally sex-role-appropriate areas by social structural and other cultural factors. Laws (1978), for example, indicates that women's employment behavior is subject to powerful external constraints, including sex discrimination and family obligations. Thus, it is not surprising that women are likely to express their achievement orientation in areas that have been traditionally defined as sex-role-appropriate.

Nevertheless, despite negative cultural sanctions and social structural constraints, many women do pursue nontraditional academic and career achievement, which suggests that they place high value on achievement in these areas. Denmark, Tangri, and McCandless (1978) note that whether a woman channels her achievement orientation into social skills or intellectual competence may depend on what activities and goals she has incorporated into her concept of femininity. In other words, assuming that most women want to comply with their own concept of femininity, a woman will be more likely to engage in intellectual pursuits if her definition of femininity includes this achievement area. The pertinent point for our study is that in light of recent changes in women's actual roles, women's concept of femininity is likely to differ among women of different cohorts, and these differences may be reflected in the channeling of achievement orientation into nontraditional versus traditional pursuits.

Thus far we have seen that women may express their achievement orientation in women's traditional roles, in academic and career pursuits, or in both areas. Since values influence task choice (Parsons & Goff 1978; Smith 1969), it would seem that attainment values would be particularly useful in predicting women's achievement behavior. Indeed, studies of children and adolescents show that attainment values predict task choice (Crandall, Katkovsky & Preston 1962), task persistence (Battle 1965), and competence (Battle 1966). Yet, research on attainment values has several important limitations. First, the subjects in most studies of attainment values have been children and adolescents. Second, researchers have demonstrated the relationship between attainment values and task choice in experimental settings, but have neglected the relationship between attainment values and long-range choices and goals (Parsons & Goff

1978). Yet, Parsons and Goff (1978) suggest that women's attainment values must be examined in order to understand their long-range choices and goals. Third, prior to the present study, researchers had not examined the systematic age and life-cycle stage changes in women's attainment values. Yet, both attitudinal and behavioral data make it reasonable to expect such generational and life-cycle shifts. The evidence that suggests such shifts in women's attainment values and the behavioral expression of attainment values through career and family will be reviewed in a subsequent section of this chapter.

In addition to the area of expression of achievement orientation, various theorists and researchers have considered the mode of expression of achievement orientation. Parsons and Goff (1978), for example, draw upon Bakan's (1966) two global approaches to life, known as "agentic" and "communal," to describe types of achievement orientation. "Agentic achievement" is characterized by protection of self, assertion, and mastery, while "communal achievement" is characterized by the desire to be with rather than apart from others, and to gain rewards through interaction rather than through competition with others. Parsons and Goff (1978) suggest, further, that women typically conform to the communal mode of achievement, which tends to integrate the achievement and affiliation motives, while men typically conform to the agentic style, which tends to segregate these two motives. Furthermore, they argue that affiliative factors should be incorporated within the traditional model of achievement orientation.

Other social scientists have also developed typologies related to the mode in which achievement orientation is expressed. In the original conceptualization of achievement motivation, achievement was defined in terms of the individual's own effort and performance. Lipman-Blumen and Leavitt (1977), however, distinguish between direct and vicarious orientations toward achievement. They further differentiate among three types of vicarious achievement, all of which involve obtaining some type of gratification for one's own achievement needs through the achievement behavior of another individual. In the altruistic vicarious type of achievement orientation, satisfaction is derived simply from association with the direct achiever. The contributing vicarious achiever derives satisfaction from actually assisting or in some way facilitating another's direct achievement. The instrumental vicarious achiever uses the relationship with the direct achiever as a means to some other end, such as status or influence.

Three types of direct achievement orientation are also identified (Lipman-Blumen & Leavitt 1977). Intrinsic direct achievement orientation, in which the goal of the achiever's behavior is task mastery or attainment of a standard of excellence, closely resembles the achievement motive as initially conceptualized. This type of direct achievement orientation may be distinguished from the competitive and instrumental types, in which the goal is, respectively, to outdo others and to use achievement as a means to other ends.

Women's traditional family roles are generally associated with vicarious, rather than direct, achievement. Coser and Rokoff (1971) note that women must attain their social status vicariously, since opportunities to achieve status directly have generally been closed to them. As wives and mothers, women may facilitate and obtain vicarious satisfaction from the achievements of their husbands and children. Furthermore, the types of occupations into which women have been typically directed place them in nurturing, supporting roles resembling their family roles and conducive to vicarious achievement. Thus, in preparation for the roles society assigns them, the differential socialization of girls and boys has encouraged the tendency to adopt vicarious and direct achievement orientations, respectively (Lipman-Blumen & Leavitt 1977). Yet, women may achieve directly, not just vicariously, in both family and occupational roles.

Thus, although both the area and the mode of expression of women's achievement orientation tend to be sex role-related, the two dimensions (area and mode) are independent. Both direct and vicarious achievement are possible within family, career, and other areas. Troll (1975:56) presents a typology showing examples of direct and indirect (vicarious) expression of women's achievement motivation. Included in the schema are four different achievement concepts, or definitions of achievement, that reflect the multidimensionality of achievement motivation: task mastery, recognition or status, interpersonal influence, and creativity. Morever, her schema gives examples of the direct expression of achievement motivation in three areas: home and community, sex-typed "feminine" jobs, and role-innovative "masculine" jobs. Although Troll does not include examples of vicarious achievement in all three of these areas, it would be possible to devise such examples, illustrating that vicarious achievement, as well as direct achievement, is possible in both family and occupational roles.

Thus we see that in the study of women and achievement, it is important to consider variations in the expression of achievement orientation. In the present study, the available data allowed us to assess the area, but not the mode, of expression of women's achievement orientation. The study tests the hypothesis that the level of women's achievement orientation is stable across generations and life-cycle stages, but that the expression of achievement orientation, through career and family, varies among women of different generations, life-cycle stages, and life-course patterns.

STABILITY IN THE LEVEL OF WOMEN'S ACHIEVEMENT ORIENTATION

Very little research has been addressed to the issue of stability versus change in women's achievement orientation across the life cycle and across cohorts. In its initial conceptualization, achievement motivation was posited as a relatively stable disposition (Stein & Bailey 1976). Indeed, two longitudinal studies (Kagan & Moss 1962; Crandall & Battle 1970) found correlations in female achievement motivation in childhood, adolescence, and early adulthood.

Yet, Baruch (1967) posited a temporal cycle in women's achievement motivation related to age and family status. Achievement motivation was expected to decline during the period of family expansion, then rise when the family was completed. Moreover, after family completion, she expected a significant relationship between high achievement motivation and return to paid employment.

Using a projective measure of achievement motivation (Atkinson 1958), Baruch (1967) first tested her hypothesis in a cross-sectional sample of Radcliffe alumnae who were 5, 10, 15, 20, and 25 years out of college. The hypothesis was supported. Achievement motivation was lowest among women in the childbearing years, significantly higher when the family was completed, and stable thereafter. Furthermore, there was a significant association between achievement motivation and paid employment among the women 20 and 25 years out of college. In a replication of this study in a nationally representative sample, Baruch (1967) found the Radcliffe pattern of achievement motivation only among women who had attended college. A slightly different pattern of decline and rise in achievement motivation existed among the high school graduates; and among those who did not complete high school, achievement motivation declined with age.

To summarize, the results of Baruch's analysis of the Radcliffe sample suggest a pattern of life-cycle changes in achievement motivation. The findings suggest that achievement motivation declines during the early child-rearing years, and rises thereafter, at least among college-educated women. We argue, however, that the findings of Baruch's study may have resulted from failure to distinguish, in methodology and assumptions, between changes in the level of achievement motivation and in the way achievement motivation is expresed.

Part of the basis for Baruch's (1967) hypothesis of a temporal cycle in women's achievement motivation was the observation of a temporal cycle in their career patterns. Furthermore, her second hypothesis of a rise in achievement motivation followed by a return to paid employment was an attempt to explain women's labor force patterns in terms of achievement needs. There are several problems with such an approach.

First, while the need for achievement is an increasingly important motivation for women's employment (see Dubnoff, Veroff & Kulka 1978, cited in Hoffman 1979), to assume a direct link between achievement need and employment ignores the variety of ways that women's achievement needs can be met in the home and in other nonoccupational areas. Furthermore, the employment patterns that Baruch observed have changed somewhat since the time of her study. Although women's labor force participation is still linked to the family life cycle (see Taeuber & Sweet 1976; U.S. Department of Commerce, Bureau of the Census 1980), women are increasingly likely to maintain continuous labor force participation even during the most demanding family stages (Huston-Stein & Higgins-Trenk 1978). Indeed, structural

factors both encourage and limit women's labor force participation (see Zellman 1976) in such a way that the extent to
which achievement orientation is expressed through employment is not entirely a matter of individual choice. It can
even be argued that women's career activity and employment
patterns are more strongly related to structural and societal
factors than to individual psychological factors. At any rate,
one cannot assume that there is a particularly strong, direct
relationship between women's achievement orientation and
their labor force participation, especially at this point in
history.

But beyond this problem in basic assumptions, the
Baruch study was also limited in its methodology. Baruch
(1967) used a projective measure of achievement motivation
that was based on an early conceptualization of achievement
motivation and focused on leadership and intellectual endeavors. On the basis of early studies, the validity of this
measure for women has been questioned (Denmark, Tangri &
McCandless 1978). Baruch (1967) did in fact recognize the
general limitations of the available achievement motivation
measures for female populations. Nevertheless, since Radcliffe graduates can be assumed to place a high value on
intellectual attainment, she suggested that the achievement
motivation measures were valid for her sample. This assumption, however, does not allow for changes in the way
achievement motivation is expressed. Thus, the age differences in level of achievement motivation that were observed in the Radcliffe sample may reflect a decline and rise
in the value attached to direct intellectual achievement
rather than changes in the general level of achievement need.
And the association between high achievement motivation
and return to paid employment among the older women may
reflect the effects of social structural factors, including
changes in family demands and responsibilities, on the channeling and expression of achievement motivation. In general,
measures that are not sensitive to variations in the expression of achievement orientation may not accurately assess its
level. Thus, our basic argument is that the general need to
achieve remains stable across the life cycle, while the areas
in which achievement is valued and the mode of achievement
may change.

As with the study of life-cycle fluctuations in the level
of achievement motivation, little research has focused on

generational changes in the level of women's achievement motivation. Nevertheless, Troll (1975) reports the results of one pertinent study (Troll et al. 1969) that compared the achievement motivation of college students and their parents. In that study, the correlation between the achievement motivations of fathers and sons (.45) was higher than the mother–daughter correlation (.30). Troll (1975) concludes that this study suggests that there have been historical shifts in the level of women's achievement motivation.

Furthermore, Stein and Bailey (1976) suggest that the Baruch (1967) study, discussed above, may reflect generational changes in women's achievement motivation. They point out that because Baruch's data were cross-sectional (gathered at one point in time) rather than longitudinal (gathered at two or more points in time), the observed differences in levels of achievement motivation may be due to generational changes rather than changes over the life cycle.

Bardwick (1971), however, argues that any historical changes in women's achievement motivation are at most minimal, and she offers several explanations for Baruch's finding of particularly high achievement motivation among women who have been out of college 15 years. The first is Baruch's (1967) own explanation, focusing on the reemergence of a preexisting motive to achieve that was suppressed during the early years of marriage. Bardwick's second explanation is that the motive to achieve may develop later in life for many women, after affiliation needs are met through, for example, a stable marriage. But most pertinent to the discussion here, Bardwick also notes that women's motives to achieve may emerge in traditional activities as well as in paid employment. The point is congruent with our basic contention that women's achievement motivation may be expressed through the family as well as career activities.

This brief review shows that although some have argued that there are life–cycle and generational changes in the level of women's achievement motivation, the evidence to support these assertions is not compelling. Thus, we maintain that the level of women's achievement orientation (need to achieve) is stable, but that its expression, through career and family, varies across generations and life–cycle stages.

VARIATIONS IN THE EXPRESSION OF
WOMEN'S ACHIEVEMENT ORIENTATION

Both behavioral and attitudinal data suggest generational shifts in the areas in which women express their achievement orientation. More specifically, the data suggest generational transitions both in the values that women attach to achievement in the areas of career and family--that is, shifts in attainment values--and in the extent to which career values are expressed through participation in paid employment. Several changes suggest this recent generational shift toward higher career values among younger women:

First, structural and ideological changes, including a recent emphasis on equality of opportunity and affirmative action, encourage women's career development (Zellman 1976).

Second, changes in employment rates and patterns among adult women suggest a heightening of career interest, as recent cohorts of women have shown higher labor force participation rates at each life-cycle stage (Taeuber & Sweet 1976). At the same time, recent reports indicate that the need for achievement may be an increasingly important factor in women's employment. The results of national surveys reveal that the proportion of women who cited achievement satisfactions as reasons for working increased from 1 percent in 1957 to 10 percent in 1976 (Dubnoff, Veroff & Kulka 1978, cited in Hoffman 1979).

Finally, attitude surveys reveal rapidly increasing career aspirations among successive cohorts of adolescent and college women, accompanied by a decreasing willingness to focus exclusively on the homemaker role (Cross 1975; Tangri 1972; see also Bernard 1975).

In addition to this evidence, several trends suggest a decline in the channeling of achievement orientation into the family. Data suggest that women's involvement in family and maternal roles has declined since about 1960: "women are more likely to remain single in early adulthood, they marry later, they have fewer children, and they have their children later" (Huston-Stein & Higgins-Trenk 1978:264). These behavioral trends are supported by attitudinal data showing a decline in the expected family size of young women (Huston-Stein & Higgins-Trenk 1978:265) and an increase in the proportion of young women who expect to remain childless (Bram 1974, cited in Huston-Stein & Higgins-Trenk 1978:265).

Nevertheless, the importance of the family to women should not be underestimated. Recent data suggest marriage is still a major concern and important goal for many young women (see Bernard 1981). And surveys show that young women in college generally expect to have both marriage and a career, not just marriage or career alone (see, e.g., Cross 1975; Komarovsky 1973). Moreover, the data suggest that among career-oriented women who delay childbearing, child rearing is still a critical concern and an important arena for achievement once the first child is born (see, e.g., Fabe & Wikler 1979).

As with generational differences, there is considerable evidence suggesting that the areas in which women value achievement (that is, their attainment values) vary among women of different life-cycle stages and life-course patterns. Moreover, there is evidence that the extent to which women's attainment values are expressed in actual behavior varies among women of different life-cycle stages and life-course patterns.

In understanding these variations, two factors are important. First, various structural incentives and constraints, including the structures of employing institutions, as well as family and household responsibilities and demands, strongly affect women's choice of family and career roles (Laws 1978). Second, there are reciprocal effects of individual values and roles. A woman's values may affect her choice of roles, but the enactment of a role, whether from choice or constraint, can reinforce or produce the attitudes and values that are congruent with it (see Aronson 1980; Berger 1963; Huston-Stein & Higgins-Trenk 1978). There is a psychological "push" toward congruence between one's attitudes and behavior, and behavior change often precedes attitude change. Whether consciously or not, individuals tend to adjust their attitudes to fit their behavior (see Aronson 1980). It should be noted, however, that the process that operates to produce congruence between attitudes and behavior is far from perfect, and the notion of individual freedom implies that it is possible to maintain attitudes and values that are discrepant with the roles one is constrained, or has chosen, to play (see Berger 1963).

These theoretical points suggest that the values women attach to achievement through family versus career are likely to change as they move through the different stages of the family life cycle, and into and out of the labor force. Moreover, women who follow different life-course patterns--a never-married woman who is employed throughout her adult life, compared with a woman who marries young and follows the typical family life-cycle pattern--are likely to attach differing values to family versus career achievement. Finally, various discrepancies are likely to arise between women's values and the roles that they play, partially as a result of structural constraints and incentives that influence role enactment, and these discrepancies are likely to be greater at some stages of the life cycle than at others.

Empirical evidence supports the hypothesis of life-course differences and life-cycle changes in attainment values. First, research has shown that among girls, achievement motivation is expressed differently during different developmental stages (Lesser 1973). It is thus reasonable to expect life-cycle changes in the expression of achievement motivation during adulthood as well.

Second, research has shown that during the college years, young women's occupational choices and career plans are sometimes made contingent on their marriage and family plans (Angrist & Almquist 1975). If career plans thus change as young women anticipate family role responsibilities, then the actual demands of marriage and motherhood, at subsequent life stages, are likely to have an even greater effect on career and family values.

Third, the results of several studies suggest a developmental pattern in which the enactment of the career role produces or reinforces positive career attitudes (see, e.g., Feldman 1973; U.S. Department of Labor, Women's Bureau 1966). Early adulthood seems to be a critical period for the operation of this process and the determination of subsequent employment plans and behavior (Huston-Stein & Higgins-Trenk, 1978).

Fourth, research suggests that creative child rearing is regarded as an arena for achievement among many highly educated women (Veroff & Feld 1970; Bardwick 1971). Thus, the much-discussed return to work and to school among older mothers (see, e.g., Bernard 1975, 1981) may represent not a rise in achievement motivation, but a rechanneling of its expression when satisfactions from mothering decline.

Finally, studies of young women beyond college suggest that despite some degree of stability in work commitment, actual career plans and employment behavior are never-theless related to marital and parental status (see Eyde 1968; U.S. Department of Labor, Women's Bureau 1966). More-over, despite increased labor force participation among women of all ages and life-cycle stages, national statistics show that women's employment rates and patterns are still closely linked to the family life cycle (U.S. Department of Commerce, Bureau of the Census 1980). For example, employment rates are higher among single and childless women than among married women and mothers, and rates are lowest among mothers of infants and preschoolers (U.S. Department of Commerce, Bureau of the Census 1980). We must exercise caution, however, in interpreting these em-ployment statistics as evidence for life-course differences and life-cycle stage changes in women's attainment values; employment rates may reflect not only the expression of achievement orientation but also a variety of structural constraints, incentives, and personal motivations.

Empirical evidence also suggests that there are dis-continuities between women's career values and the be-havioral expression of career values through paid employ-ment. Retrospective studies of middle-aged women reveal discrepancies between women's employment patterns and both their current work values (Mulvey 1963) and their vocational interests during college (Harmon 1967). The discrepancies between career attitudes and employment pat-terns found in these studies could be interpreted as indicating that women's career values change over time, as was dis-cussed above. The findings of these studies may also be interpreted, however, as suggesting discontinuities in the expression of women's career values through employment. Among other reasons, these discontinuities may arise as a result of the value or importance that women assign to other, competing areas, such as the family (Parsons & Goff 1978), or as a result of various structural constraints, including family responsibilities and job discrimination (Laws 1978). More-over, we expect that the degree of the discrepancy between career values and employment behavior will vary among women of different generations, life-cycle stages, and life-course patterns.

To summarize, the present study represents a social structural approach to the study of women's achievement orientation. Unlike prior research, we maintain that structural variables, including age and marital and parental status, partially determine women's achievement values and behavior, but not the level of their achievement orientation across adulthood. Essentially, the present study suggests that it is primarily the structural variables defining generation, life-cycle stage, and life-course pattern that ultimately channel the expression of women's achievement orientation, thus determining their career activity and employment patterns.

WORK, FAMILY, AND LIFE SATISFACTION

As we have seen, recent, rapid social changes in women's career and family roles have been accompanied by important transitions in women's attitudes toward career and family. And, individually, women's attitudes toward career and family are likely to change as they move through various transitions in the life cycle. These observations raise an important question: How does the relationship between a woman's objective roles and her subjective attitudes, or values, regarding these roles affect her overall life satisfaction?

Prior research has focused primarily on the effects of structural variables, rather than on the combination of structural and psychological variables, on women's well-being. Indeed, during recent decades many researchers have sought to determine how the structural conditions of work and family statuses affect the well-being of women at various ages and life-cycle stages.* In general, these studies have shown that marital, parental, and employment status interact with such variables as age, educational and occupational levels, and socioeconomic status in predicting both mental health and life satisfaction (see, e.g., Birnbaum 1975; Campbell et al. 1976; Meile et al. 1976; Nye 1974; Sears & Barbee 1977; Spreitzer et al. 1975). Moreover, changes in satisfaction are associated with changes in roles as a person moves through the life course (Campbell 1981). Thus, research suggests that satisfaction depends, to some extent, on the total configuration of a person's statuses and roles.

---

*The findings of many of these studies, focusing on the effects of marital, parental, and employment status on women's well-being at various ages and life-cycle stages, will be discussed at appropriate points in the subsequent chapters.

Yet, women vary not only in their objective roles and statuses, but also in their subjective experience of, and attraction to, the roles of wife, mother, and paid worker. As we have seen, research suggests that women differ regarding the importance, or value, they attach to career and family pursuits. Not surprisingly, then, researchers have recently acknowledged the limitations of structural variables alone in explaining levels of mental health (Campbell 1975; Kanter 1977). And Campbell (1975) suggests that satisfaction depends in part on whether an individual's life circumstances are congruent with his or her subjective expectations and aspirations.

Congruence, or "goodness-of-fit," between objective roles and subjective values is particularly pertinent to a consideration of women's well-being. Earlier we noted that the relationship between women's values and roles is reciprocal. Thus, for example, a woman's attitudes toward family and career may initially affect her choice of roles, but after roles are selected, they affect the further development of attitudes and values. This is an example of the more general relationship between an individual's values and his or her position in the social structure.

To some extent, individual values reflect, and are a function of, position in the social structure (Berger 1963). Indeed, as noted earlier, people often adjust their attitudes and values in accordance with the reality of their social situations (Aronson 1980). Nevertheless, changes in values can precede, and even effect, social structural change (Berger 1963). Thus, discrepancies can arise when either values or structures remain stable relative to changes in the other.

In times of rapid social change, values and role opportunities may change at different rates in various population subgroups. Thus, over the past several decades, the values of some groups of women have changed more rapidly than structural opportunities, while for others, values have remained more stable than structures. For example, despite rising career aspirations among successive cohorts of young women (Cross 1975), structural barriers continue to impede women's participation and advancement in professional careers (Zellman 1976). At the same time, however, women's large-scale movement into the labor force, and the accompanying emphasis on career achievement for women, run counter to the values of some women who prefer full-time homemaking (Bardwick 1979; Bernard 1975).

But regardless of whether a discrepancy arises from changes in values or in structures, it is important to assess how the gap between expectations and reality affects women's well-being. By considering the interacting effects of objective situation and subjective values, we may be better able to predict the changes in life satisfaction that are likely to occur among women as they experience various transitions in the individual and family life cycles. The formulation of policies and strategies to relieve situational stress and enhance women's well-being is contingent upon an understanding of the joint effects of subjective expectations and objective opportunities.

The present study thus analyzes women's well-being as a function of both objective status and subjective value orientation. It helps to explain why women's mental health is especially "at risk" during particular life-cycle stages—because of a poor fit between work and family values and role opportunities. The analysis shows how life satisfaction depends on the availability of structural opportunities for the expression of individual values. Hence, the findings suggest the importance of structural changes designed to enhance the fit between values and opportunities, and thus alleviate the health-endangering conditions at critical life-cycle stages.

SUMMARY

The present study proposes three primary hypotheses regarding women in transition. First, it proposes that the level of women's achievement orientation is relatively stable, across generations of women and across the life course of individual women. Second, it hypothesizes that the expression of women's achievement orientation, through career and family, varies among women of different generations, life-cycle stages, and life-course patterns. Finally, it proposes that life satisfaction depends on the degree of congruence between a woman's career and family values and role opportunities. In other words, the effects of marital, parental, and employment status on a woman's well-being are partly determined by the relative value or importance that she attaches to achievement through family or career.

This chapter has provided an overview of the evidence supporting these three major hypotheses. In the following chapters we will test and discuss these hypotheses. Chapter 2 introduces the women in transition--more than 1,000 women who comprise the study group--and describes the method of the study. Chapters 3 through 6 test the study hypotheses by examining variations in achievement orientation, attainment values, and life satisfaction that exist among women of different cohorts, life-cycle stages, and life-course patterns. Chapter 3 focuses primarily on generational transitions associated with social change. Chapters 4, 5, and 6 focus on the life-cycle transitions and life-course patterns of women in different age groups. Chapter 7 summarizes and discusses the findings and implications of the study.

2.

A STUDY OF WOMEN
IN TRANSITION

LOCATING WOMEN IN TRANSITION:
THE STUDY GROUP

The women in this study are a particular group of women in transition: 1,120 women who contacted the University of Michigan Center for Continuing Education of Women (CEW) between 1964 and 1973. Because women contacting the Center are often anticipating or experiencing some type of life transition--in the area of education, work, or family-- they are particularly appropriate for the focus of this study on generational and life-cycle transitions.

In the early 1960s, continuing education programs for women began to emerge "to facilitate the entry or reentry of women past the traditional age of 18 into the academic world" (Astin 1977:139). One of the first, the University of Michigan Center was founded in 1964 specifically "to help adult women whose educations have been interrupted--most often through marriage and family--to return to college and complete degrees" (McGuigan 1978:1). Details concerning the founding of the Center, its mission, growth, services, and clientele, are summarized in The University of Michigan Center for Continuing Education of Women, 1964-1977: A Report, edited by Dorothy McGuigan and published in 1978.

Under the sponsorship of the Ford Foundation, in 1977 the Center conducted the first of a two-part questionnaire study of women in transition from education to employment. Women who were Center participants during its first ten years of operation were the subjects of this study, which was designed to "examine the nature and consequences of this transition" (Manis & Markus 1978). The first mailed questionnaire included a number of attitudinal measures, as well as sections on family background, educational and employment history, and marital and family status.

An attempt was made to locate all of the women who had contacted the Center from 1964 to 1973. A "contact," in the sense used here, entailed at least one appointment with a counselor and completion of a participant form, which requests information concerning the respondent's background, current goals, and purpose in visiting the Center.

Almost 2,000 women were located and sent a questionnaire. Of these, 1,145, or 60 percent, responded. Telephone contacts with some of the nonrespondents in the Ann Arbor area revealed that they resembled the respondents in terms of marital status and return to school. Slightly more of the respondents than nonrespondents were currently working (73 percent and 60 percent, respectively) and were career-oriented (75 percent of the respondents, compared with 69 percent of the nonrespondents, thought of themselves as having or planning a career).

During the years covered by this study, the demographic profile of the average Center participant changed somewhat. In 1964-65, a woman contacting the Center was likely to be married, in her middle to late thirties, and the mother of two or three children. Her educational attainment at the time of contact was generally a bachelor's degree, or at least some college. The primary goal of this early participant was preparation for paid employment, and she came to the Center for help in considering job possibilities and in choosing and beginning an appropriate educational program. A gradual shift in the Center's population during the early 1970s resulted in an average participant who was markedly younger and quite likely to be single, divorced, or widowed. The typical participant's goal, however, remained essentially unchanged. She was, and is today, interested in gaining admission to and completing an educational program that is suitable to her occupational goals. Throughout the Center's history, few participants have cited noncredit study, self-improvement, or volunteer work as their primary goals (Campbell 1973). Thus, although varied in social structural position, the population from which the sample for this study was drawn was relatively homogeneous in purpose at the time of contact with the Center.

Of the total respondents in the Center's study, this analysis of women in transition is limited to those between the ages of 22 and 64, inclusive. Because the CEW sample was not selected randomly, it may be useful to compare it with a more representative sample of U.S. women. In fact, compared with a national probability sample, the CEW study group includes a larger proportion of white, married, highly educated, and relatively affluent women.

The particular characteristics of the CEW sample have several important implications for our focus on age and life-cycle stage differences in women's achievement orientation and life satisfaction. Because of their educational attainment and affluence, the women in our sample are more likely than women in the general population to have access to meaningful and well-paying jobs, and to have the freedom to reject boring or distasteful tasks and working conditions. Essentially, then, our sample roughly controls, or holds constant, such important structural factors as educational and occupational level, working conditions, and socioeconomic status. As a result, the effects of cohort membership and life-cycle stage on the expression of achievement orientation should be more clearly evident. Moreover, we can more readily see how achievement values mediate the relationship between a woman's family and employment statuses and her life satisfaction.

CHARACTERIZING THE WOMEN IN TRANSITION:
DEMOGRAPHIC VARIABLES

Women's lives are different depending upon when they were born, whether they are married, whether they are mothers (and if so, the ages of their children), and whether they are employed. These variables--age, marital and parental status, and employment status--help to locate a woman's position in the social structure. In the present study, we are interested in the variations in women's lives that are associated with these different positions in the social structure, and with variations in the timing of marriage and motherhood.

In order to analyze these various life patterns, we first categorize the sample according to age, marital status, and parental status. Approximately one-third of the sample is included in each of three age cohorts: 22-34, 35-44, and 45-64. In turn, each cohort consists of five life-cycle groups defined by marital status and age of youngest child. Table 2.1 lists, for each cohort, the percentage of women within each life-cycle group.

Each of the resulting 15 life-cycle groups represents a distinct combination of age, marital status, and parental status, and thus reflects a unique position in the social structure. As a whole, however, the 15 groups do not represent a series of progressive stages in the individual or family life-cycle. Instead, they reflect a diversity of life-course patterns with respect to marital status, parental status, and the timing of marriage and childbearing. Thus, this categorization enables us to examine the variations in women's life-course patterns associated with differences in cohort membership, marital and parental status, and the timing of marriage and motherhood.

Each woman in the sample was further characterized according to her employment status: employed full-time, employed part-time, or not employed at all.

Age cohort, life-cycle group, and employment status describe a woman's position in the larger social structure. To some extent, these external factors shape and influence a woman's attitudes and feelings--her interior life. We turn now to the problem of assessing these internal characteristics.

CHARACTERIZING THE WOMEN IN TRANSITION:
ATTITUDINAL VARIABLES

Our study requires that we devise measures for four specific types of attitudes, dispositions, or feelings: achievement orientation, career and family attainment values, career orientation, and life satisfaction.

Table 2.1. Percentage of Respondents by Life–Cycle Groups Within Age Cohorts

Life–Cycle Group	Percent
Age Cohort: 22–34	
Single childless women	23.95
Married childless women	17.89
Married mothers of preschool children	34.74
Married mothers of elementary school children	14.47
Single mothers	8.95
Total percent	100.00
(N)	(380)
Age Cohort: 35–44	
Married mothers of preschool children	8.99
Married mothers of elementary school children	43.60
Married mothers of adolescent and adult children	21.25
Single mothers	15.26
Childless women[a]	10.90
Total percent	100.00
(N)	(367)
Age Cohort: 45–64	
Married mothers of children and adolescents	34.32
Married mothers of adult children	41.28
Single mothers of children and adolescents	7.51
Single mothers of adult children	12.06
Childless women[b]	4.83
Total percent	100.00
(N)	(373)

[a]Two-fifths of the childless women in the 35–44 cohort are married.

[b]One-third of the childless women in the 45–64 cohort are married.

Source: From Faver (1981): Table 1. Copyright 1981 by Sage Publications, Inc. Used by permission.

Achievement Orientation and Attainment Values

Three attitude scales were constructed from Likert-type questionnaire items. The achievement orientation scale measures primarily two important components of the multi-dimensional achievement orientation concept:(1) personal efficacy and self-esteem about achievement. Two attainment values scales assess the value assigned by respondents to achievement through career and family.(2)

From these scales, three dichotomous variables were created to represent high and low achievement orientation, high and low career values, and high and low family values. The dichotomous career and family values variables were then used to construct a combined career and family values variable with four levels: high on both career and family values; high on career values, low on family values; low on family values, high on career values; low on both career and family values. The combined variable thus provides a single measure assessing the relative importance of career and family to each respondent. The Appendix shows the questionnaire items and scoring procedure for the three scales, and describes the construction of the dichotomous variables.

Career Orientation

Career orientation is a dichotomous variable (career-oriented versus not career-oriented) based on the responses to the following questionnaire item:

> Would you describe yourself as having long-range employment or career goals--that is, do you think in terms of not just a "job" but of working the rest of your life, in a specific field or type of work, developing and using skills necessary for that field?
> ___Yes, I do think of myself as having or planning a career.
> ___No, I do not think of myself as having or planning a career.

An important distinction must be made between career orientation and career values. The measure of career orientation assesses whether a woman regards herself as having, or intending to have, a career. The measure of career values, in contrast, assesses the degree of importance a woman attaches to her career.

Life Satisfaction

Life satisfaction is a continuous, intervally scaled variable measuring the extent to which a woman agrees that her life is currently interesting and satisfying.(3) The questionnaire item and scoring procedure used for this variable are shown in the Appendix.

ANALYZING THE WOMEN IN TRANSITION: THE STUDY PLAN

There are essentially two focuses in our analysis of women in transition. First, we examine age cohort and life-cycle group variance in achievement orientation, career orientation, career and family values, and employment status, and in various relationships among these variables. In these tasks our primary tools are contingency tables, the chi-square test, and several measures of assocation. From this analysis we will draw inferences regarding differences in women's achievement attitudes and behavior that may be associated with generational and life-cycle transitions, and with variations in the timing of life-course events. Because the data are cross-sectional, we cannot make definitive distinctions among generational, life-cycle, and timing effects. Nevertheless, comparing women in the same age cohort but different family life-cycle stages, and in the same life-cycle stage but different age cohorts, will help us to make some tentative inferences concerning the source of observed differences.

The second part of the analysis focuses on the relative life satisfaction of women of varying objective statuses and subjective value orientations. One-way analysis of variance is used to test for significant differences in the mean life satisfaction scores of women who vary in marital status, employment status, or life-cycle group. In these analyses, the dichotomous career and family values variables are used as control variables. This enables us to examine the relationship between work or family status and life satisfaction for women of different value orientations; in addition, a measure of association, eta-square, is used to assess the strength of these relationships. In this way, we consider the ways in which discrepancies between objective status and subjective values affect satisfaction levels.

Chapters 3 through 6 discuss the findings of these analyses. We focus upon comparisons among women in different age cohorts (Chapter 3); in the same cohort but different life-cycle stages (Chapters 4-6); and in the same life-cycle stage but different cohorts (Chapters 4-6). These comparisons make it possible to differentiate tentatively between life-cycle and generational transitions; to discuss differences among women who are "on time" or "off time" (Neugarten 1977) in moving through the family life cycle; and to compare women who are moving through the traditional family life cycle with those who are following nontraditional, but increasingly prevalent patterns, such as single motherhood, delayed childbearing, or childlessness.

NOTES

1. For a discussion of the multiple components and factors in achievement orientation, see Veroff et al. (1975).

2. Construct validity of the three scales is established in Faver (1979).

3. For the sample as a whole, the distribution on this variable is skewed toward relatively high satisfaction. In this respect, the CEW respondents resemble the respondents in Campbell's (1975) national probability sample, the majority of whom reported relatively high satisfaction. Nevertheless, our measure makes significant differentiations in the satisfaction levels of women who vary in value orientations and in marital, parental, and employment status.

3.

GENERATIONAL TRANSITION: A COMPARISON OF AGE COHORTS

The women in the three age cohorts of this study grew up under different historical circumstances (see Troll 1975:10), and thus experienced different "worlds" or "cultures" during their early years of socialization (see Bernard 1981:127). The women in the oldest cohort, aged 45-64 in 1977, were born between 1913 and 1932. Depending on whether they were born early or late during this period, their early childhood was marked by World War I or the depression of the 1930s. The middle cohort (35-44), born between 1933 and 1942, were children of the late depression and World War II. Because of the low birthrate of the 1930s, women who were about 35 to 50 years old in 1977 have been termed a "hollow generation" (Bernard 1981:127), a term that would cover all of the women in our middle cohort, as well as the younger women in the oldest cohort. Our youngest cohort (25-34), born between 1943 and 1952, were in their early childhood during the years immediately following World War II and during the family-oriented, "feminine mystique" (Friedan 1963) period of the 1950s.

We may expect certain differences in attitudes among these three cohorts. Studies show, for example, that compared with younger women, older women tend to be less supportive of the ideology of the women's movement (Bernard 1975: ch.8). As Bernard (1981:127) explains: "Older women reflect a world of the past. We expect them to be living in a more conservative world than younger women."

Although older people do alter their attitudes in conjunction with social change, they still remain more traditional in their views than younger people (Bernard 1975:ch. 8). In general, the effects of cultural change on adults seem to depend on their life stage (Huston-Stein & Higgins-Trenk 1978:260). Even in the face of social change, older people may be less likely to adopt new roles and values because they "have made life choices about childbearing and work that are not reversible" (Huston-Stein & Higgins-Trenk 1978:262). In other words, older women "were reared in a different world and they cling to it" (Bernard 1981:127).

In its effect on career and family attitudes, a particularly significant aspect of childhood is the mother's employment status. Daughters of unemployed mothers are more career-oriented and have more liberal attitudes toward women's roles (see Huston-Stein & Higgins-Trenk 1978:279-80). And, as we noted earlier, large-scale entrance of women into the labor force occurred during World War II (Chafe 1976). Thus, the younger women in our sample are more likely to have been influenced by the presence of an employed mother as a role model.

In general, then, we would expect the women in our oldest cohort to be more family-oriented, and those in the youngest cohort to be more career-oriented. Those in the middle cohort may be considered a transition generation. Indeed, the older women in this middle cohort may resemble a "swing generation" of women who reflect both traditional and modern attitudes, values, and behaviors (see Bernard 1981:127-28).

By comparing women in the three age cohorts of our sample, this chapter begins to analyze primarily generational, but also life-cycle, transitions in the expression of women's achievement orientation. We examine the evidence for stability in level of achievement orientation, but variation in the expression of achievement orientation through career and family, across the three cohorts. Moreover, we consider whether, for the sample as a whole, life satisfaction is related not to chronological age, but to the degree of congruence between the individual's values and role opportunities.

ACHIEVEMENT ORIENTATION

Without both longitudinal and cross-sectional data, it is impossible to test directly the hypothesis of stability in achievement orientation. Nevertheless, these cross-sectional data show that the proportion of women with high achievement orientation does not vary significantly across age cohorts (Table 3.1). This suggests generational and life-course stability, rather than change, in level of achievement orientation. In subsequent chapters, life-cycle group comparisons will be used as a further test of the hypothesis of stability in achievement orientation during adulthood.

As was noted in Chapter 1, two longitudinal studies (Kagan & Moss 1962; Crandall & Battle 1970) found correlations in female achievement motivation in childhood, adolescence, and early adulthood. Considered together, those two earlier studies and the present study suggest that achievement orientation is stable across the life course.

Nevertheless, our findings thus far are somewhat at variance with those of Baruch (1967), whose results suggested significant fluctuations in achievement orientation during early and middle adulthood. The two studies, however, are not directly comparable. While Baruch used a projective measure of achievement motivation, our study uses a more general scale of achievement orientation.

Moreover, a difference in findings may be related to differences between the two samples in terms of the timing of education. Baruch (1967) observed that achievement motivation is partly a product of intellectual stimulation in the environment. Thus, decline in achievement motivation may be associated with distance from intellectual stimulation. Since she tested a sample who had completed college at the normative point in the life cycle, age was almost perfectly correlated with years since college completion. In the CEW sample, however, this correlation is not as strong, since many of these women returned to school during adulthood. Thus, this difference in the relationship between age and time away from college may be a source of difference in findings from the two samples.

Table 3.1. Achievement Orientation, Career Values, and Family Values, by Age Cohort (percentage distribution)

	Dichotomous Variables (percent ranking high)		
Age Cohort	High Achievement Orientation (Percent)[a]	High Career Values (Percent)[b]	High Family Values (Percent)[c]
22–34	62.8	78.5	44.8
35–44	64.5	66.7	58.3
45–64	59.9	51.3	65.9
χ^2 [d]	1.67	59.64*	32.02*
Goodman-Kruskal γ [e]	-.0409	-.3928	.2829

[a]Mean scores on the achievement orientation scale for the 22–34, 35–44, and 45–64 cohorts are, respectively, 4.22, 4.25, and 4.21 (F = .605, N.S.).

[b]Mean scores on the career values scale for the 22–34, 35–44, and 45–64 cohorts are, respectively, 3.87, 3.56, and 3.11 (F = 47.08, p< .0001).

[c]Mean scores on the family values scale for the 22–34, 35–44, and 45–64 cohorts are, respectively, 2.99, 3.31, and 3.53 (F = 25.84, p< .0001).

[d]The χ^2 (chi-square) statistics test the significance of the association between age cohort and each of the dichotomous variables. For each χ^2 test, df = 2.

[e]Goodman-Kruskal γ (gamma) is a measure of rank correlation (University of Michigan 1976) reflecting the degree of the relationship between age cohort and each of the dichotomous variables

*p < .0001.

CAREER ORIENTATION

Our measure of career orientation assesses whether a woman regards herself as having or planning a career, not the value or degree of importance she attaches to career pursuit. In the CEW sample, a high proportion of women in each cohort are career-oriented (the percentages are 93.2, 88.5, and 76.2, respectively, in the 22-24, 35-44, 45-64 cohorts). Nevertheless, with increasing age, the proportion of career-oriented women decreases significantly ($\chi^2 = 41.5$, p < .0001), suggesting a generational shift toward widespread career interest among young women. This finding supports prior studies that revealed marked increases in career orientation--that is, intention to pursue a career--among successive cohorts of young women (Cross 1975; Helson 1975).

ATTAINMENT VALUES

While career orientation simply indicates whether a woman has, or is planning, a career, career values assess the importance that she attaches to her career. Similarly, family values assess the importance attached to family involvement.

Our data show that with increasing age, the proportion of women with high career values decreases, and the proportion of women with high family values increases (Table 3.1). Moreover, nearly half (48.9 percent) of the 22- to 34-year-old women have high career and low family values. These findings seem to reflect a generational shift toward increasing career emphasis among young women.

Yet, age is more strongly associated with career values than with family values (Table 3.1). Furthermore, over a fourth of the women in each cohort have both high career and high family values (the percentages are 29.4, 31.16, and 26.8, respectively, in the 22-34, 35-44, and 45-64 cohorts). Thus, along with strong career concern, a sizable minority of young women are maintaining an interest in family pursuits as well. This finding supports previous studies indicating that recent cohorts of young women often do not want to substitute career for family; instead, they want both (Angrist & Almquist 1975; Bernard 1975; Cross 1975).

A generational transition in women's career and family values seems to be the most plausible explanation for our findings thus far. Paradoxically, however, the observed age cohort variance in attainment values may reflect stability, as well as change, in the social structures, institutions, and opportunities affecting women. Despite striking increases in women's labor force participation (U.S. Department of Commerce, Bureau of the Census 1980), numerous structural barriers, including educational and labor market discrimination (Astin & Bayer 1975; Van Dusen & Sheldon 1976; Zellman 1976), continue to impede women's career development. In fact, as women are actually exposed to discrimination in the labor force, their perception of discrimination increases (Gould & Pagano 1972). This perception of discrimination may be especially likely to discourage the continued career participation of women (Huston-Stein & Higgins-Trenk 1978). Moreover, regardless of their labor force participation, women still bear the major responsibility for household management and child care (Kreps & Leaper 1976). Hence, whether alone or in tandem, discrimination in the labor market and demands from home and family can strongly discourage even career-committed women from long-term career involvement. Thus, many older women in our sample may have rechanneled their achievement orientation into the family--the "legitimate" arena for female achievement--following early, direct confrontation with structurally limited prospects for career achievement.

Accordingly, the high career values of the young women in our sample may reflect an untested perception that career opportunities abound for the educationally prepared woman. For some, career aspirations may decline in the face of major structural obstacles to fulfillment. Yet, because objective opportunities have expanded somewhat, we would expect such a "disillusionment" process to diminish, but not to obliterate, an overall generational change toward the maintenance of strong career interest across the life cycle.

Nevertheless, there is still the possibility of future, age-related developmental change among the young women in our sample, since there has been a trend among recent cohorts of young women to marry at a later age and to delay childbearing (Huston-Stein & Higgins-Trenk 1978). By choice or default, some young women take up career and family roles sequentially, rather than simultaneously, beginning with a career "push" during their twenties. In fact, several studies suggest that following such early career involvement, some young women "shift gears" during their thirties and become more involved in family roles (Sheehy 1974; Scarf 1980). It is possible that such a pattern may characterize the single and childless women in our youngest cohort. If so, a shift in values is also likely to occur, with relatively more emphasis given to family values, and perhaps some diminishing of career values.

CAREER ORIENTATION, ACHIEVEMENT ORIENTATION, AND CAREER VALUES

A basic supposition of the present study is that achievement orientation, defined as a desire to meet a standard of excellence, can be directed into any particular area of endeavor. Nevertheless, highly educated, career-oriented women are likely to channel their achievement orientation into career pursuits. Thus, career orientation is related positively to achievement orientation in all three cohorts, although the positive relationship between career orientation and career values is stronger.

More important, the strength of the relationships between career orientation and both achievement orientation and career values varies across the three cohorts, revealing an interesting pattern. The relationship between career orientation and achievement orientation is similar in the two younger cohorts, but declines rather sharply among the oldest women. The relationship between career orientation and career values is also similar for the two younger cohorts. Rather than declining, however, this relationship almost doubles in strength in the 45-64 cohort.

These contrasting trends can be explained by the different effects of generation and family life-cycle stage. The declining relationship between career orientation and achievement orientation reflects the period in which the oldest women were born and experienced their childhood and early adult socialization. At that time, societal norms did not favor careers as appropriate channels of expression for women's achievement orientation. Many women thus met their achievement needs through family and volunteer activities. Even when changing norms made the career option viable, age or personal values may have prevented some women from launching a career at midlife (Bernard 1981). As a result, achievement orientation is less strongly associated with career orientation among the oldest women in the sample.

At the same time, however, the relationship between career orientation and career values is strongest among the oldest women. Life-cycle stage provides the most useful explanation of this observation. For women who have a career, the "empty nest" stage brings a relaxation of the competition between family and career demands. As the career becomes more central to self-definition, career orientation is associated with correspondingly high career values.

Thus far, the analysis has focused on attitudes and values. In the next section, we consider actual participation in the labor force.

EMPLOYMENT STATUS

Women's labor force participation depends on a number of both structural and attitudinal factors. Clearly, there have been generational changes, such that during the past "several decades, each new cohort of women has been displaying higher labor force participation rates at each life-cycle stage" (Taeuber & Sweet 1976:55). This type of effect, however, may not be readily apparent in cross-sectional analysis of women of different ages. Moreover, generational changes are tempered by the effects of marital status and family life-cycle stage. For example, single women have higher participation rates than married women, and the mothers of preschoolers have lower rates than the mothers of older children (U.S. Department of Commerce, Bureau of the Census 1980).

Educational level and family income also affect the likelihood of women's employment. Many of the CEW women are both highly educated and the wives of professional men. In fact, well-educated women are especially likely to maintain continuous employment (Huston-Stein & Higgins-Trenk 1978). Yet, while labor force participation is positively related to wives' education, it is negatively related to husband's income, when husband's income is above a certain level (Sweet 1973; U.S. Department of Labor, Women's Bureau 1975).

Considering the complex and partially conflicting effects of generation, life-cycle stage, education, and husband's income, it would be difficult to predict a woman's employment status on the basis of age alone. In the CEW sample, we have seen that with increasing age, the proportion of women who are career-oriented, and the proportion with high career values, decreases. In full-time employment rates, however, there is only slight variation across cohorts. In the 22-34, 35-44, and 45-64 cohorts, the percentages employed full-time are 43.6, 47.4, and 49.9, respectively. The discrepancies between women's employment rates and both their career orientation and their career values suggest that career intentions and interest alone are not sufficient to overcome the various structural and attitudinal constraints that inhibit women's employment.

Interestingly, despite the high educational level and strong career orientation of the CEW sample, their full-time employment rates do not differ markedly from those of women in comparable age groups in a nationally representative sample. Among women aged 22-34, 35-44, and 45-64 in the Spring 1977 General Social Survey, reported rates of full-time employment were, respectively, 47.7 percent, 43.4 percent, and 44.6 percent (1).

Numerous analyses have focused on the structural variables related to women's labor force participation (e.g., Taeuber & Sweet 1976; U.S. Department of Commerce, Bureau of the Census 1980), but relatively little is known about the attitudinal and motivational factors affecting women's employment at various life-cycle stages. Thus, we next consider the relationship of achievement needs and values to the employment status of women in our three age cohorts.

ACHIEVEMENT ORIENTATION, ATTAINMENT VALUES, AND EMPLOYMENT

Because achievement orientation can be channeled into labor force participation, we may expect a positive relationship between achievement orientation and employment status. In fact, recent reports indicate that need for achievement may be an increasingly important factor in women's employment. The results of national surveys reveal that the proportion of women who cited achievement satisfactions as reasons for working increased from 1 percent in 1957 to 10 percent in 1976 (Dubnoff, Veroff & Kulka 1978, cited in Hoffman 1979). The rising career aspirations of successive cohorts of young women (Cross 1975) provide further support for this link between achievement orientation and women's employment.

Nevertheless, because of the underutilization of their skills, many women cannot gratify their achievement needs through paid employment. And, as we have seen, women can channel their achievement orientation into other areas, including the family. Thus, the relationship between achievement orientation and employment status may be relatively weak.

Attainment values reflect the importance that women attach to achievement in specific areas. Thus, compared with achievement orientation, career and family values are likely to be much stronger predictors of women's employment activity. In general, participation in paid employment should be positively related to career values, and negatively related to family values.

Of course, if a woman regards her employment as a means of contributing to family advancement through additional income, then family values may be positively related to employment. In the present study, however, family values are defined and measured in terms of the importance attached to achievement through family formation and direct family interaction. Because outside employment would diminish the time available for direct family involvement, employment is expected to be negatively related to family values.

Yet, many women, especially young women, attach high value to both career and family. Moreover, demands from career and family vary in intensity across the life cycle. Thus, a woman's decision regarding employment may be based on a balancing of both career and family values, especially during the periods when demands from career and family compete most strongly for her time and attention.

Our analysis of the CEW sample confirms these expectations. In each cohort, there is a relatively weak, positive association between achievement orientation and employment status (Table 3.2). Moreover, compared with achievement orientation, career and family attainment values are much stronger predictors of employment status. In each

Table 3.2. χ^2 Test, Kendall's τ_b, and Goodman-Kruskal τ for Employment Status by Achievement Orientation, Career Values, and Family Values, Within Age Cohorts

	Age Cohort	χ^2 [a]	Kendall's τ_b [b]	Goodman-Kruskal τ [c]
Achievement orientation				
	22–34	4.01	.0754	.0060
	35–44	5.58**	.1151	.0096
	45–64	5.68**	.1006	.0095
Career values				
	22–34	29.15***	.2585	.0426
	35–44	24.26***	.2521	.0361
	45–64	45.90***	.3318	.0789
Family values				
	22–34	19.99***	-.1898	.0314
	35–44	25.62***	-.2563	.0444
	45–64	9.13*	-.1417	.0158

[a]Within each age cohort, χ^2 (chi-square) tests the significance of the relationship between employment status and the dichotomous achivement orientation, career values, and family values variables. For each χ^2 test, df = 2.

[b]Kendall's τ_b (tau-b) is a measure of rank correlation (University of Michigan 1976) reflecting the degree of relationship between employment status and level of achievement orientation, career values, and family values, within each cohort.

[c]Goodman-Kruskal τ(tau) is an asymmetrical measure of predictive association (University of Michigan 1976) showing the proportionate reduction in expected errors in the prediction of employment status when the achievement orientation, career values, or family values variable is used as a predictor, within each cohort.

*$p = .01$.

**$p < .01$.

***$p < .0001$.

Source: From Faver (1982a): Table 4. Copyright 1982 by Academic Press, Inc. Used by permission.

cohort, employment status is related positively to career values, and negatively to family values (Table 3.2). Career values alone are the best predictors of employment among women in the 45-64 cohort, while combined career and family values best predict employment in the two younger cohorts.

These findings suggest life-cycle stage variance in the relevance of career and family values to women's employment decisions. During the stages of family expansion and active child rearing, when career and family demands are most likely to conflict, employment decisions are based on a balancing of the relative importance attached to career and family achievement. Later, however, when opportunities for family interaction and involvement diminish, career values emerge as the more relevant and salient consideration in the decision to seek paid employment.

Of further interest is the intercohort variance in the employment status of women who have both high career and high family values. Among these women, 65.2 percent in the 45-64 cohort, compared with only 43.8 percent in the middle cohort and 36.9 percent in the 22-34 cohort, are employed full-time. The markedly higher full-time employment rate of the 45- to 64-year-old women may reflect a decline in family responsibilities during the later stages of motherhood. Nevertheless, in the two younger cohorts, almost two-fifths of the women with high career and high family values are employed part-time. This supports other research (e.g., Schwartz 1980) suggesting that for women in the early, active stages of child rearing, part-time employment may represent a means of actualizing strong career interest, at the least expense to family interaction and involvement.

Overall, our analysis suggests that attainment values may mediate the relationship between women's achievement orientation and labor force participation. Because achievement orientation can be expressed in various ways, the choice of paid employment may be a function of the relative values assigned to career activity and to other tasks and activities.

At this point, a cautionary word is necessary regarding the relationships between our attitudinal variables and women's labor force participation. Thus far, our interpretations have focused on the effects of values on employment, rather than vice versa. Technically, however, our analysis merely assesses the relative strength of achievement orientation and attainment values in predicting employment status; causal associations cannot be established with cross-sectional data. And, parenthetically, regardless of the direction of the effects, we cannot be certain that intercohort variance in the observed relationships is attributable to life-cycle stage changes.

Since attitudes and values are partially a function of position in the social structure (Berger 1963), employment and family statuses surely affect career and family values, as well as vice versa. In fact, research suggests that actual participation in paid employment can lead to increased work or career commitment (Huston-Stein & Higgins-Trenk 1978). The same may be true of family involvement. When some employed women become mothers, and experience the gratifications of the parenting role, the importance of the work role may diminish, although level of performance remains stable and actual hours worked may not decrease (Schwartz 1980).

LIFE SATISFACTION

As the review in Chapter 1 suggested, life satisfaction is affected by numerous life conditions and roles. And, although age is one factor affecting the sense of well-being, satisfaction for women is related more to transitions in life roles than to actual chronological age (Campbell 1980). Thus, not surprisingly, the women in the three age cohorts in our sample do not differ significantly in their level of life satisfaction.

Life roles, however, are related to satisfaction. In the sample as a whole, married women are significantly more satisfied with their lives than single women.(2) Yet, when we examine the relationship between marital status and satisfaction in conjunction with value orientation, a slightly different pattern emerges.

Among women with high family values, and especially among those with low career values, married women are significantly more satisfied than single women. Yet, among those with low family values or high career values, the satisfaction level of married and single women does not differ significantly (Table 3.3).

It is not surprising that marriage is important to women with high family values, since wifehood is one of women's two

Table 3.3. One-Way ANOVA of Life Satisfaction by Marital Status, by Family and Career Values

Marital Status	Mean Life Satisfaction Score	N	F-Statistic	Probability	η^2 *
		High Family Values			
Single	3.79	100	11.47	.0008	.0190
Married	4.18	495			
		Low Family Values			
Single	4.04	166	1.16	.2816	.0025
Married	4.14	297			
		High Career Values			
Single	4.05	219	3.01	.0831	.0043
Married	4.20	483			
		Low Career Values			
Single	3.43	53	19.79	<.0001	.0513
Married	4.14	353			

* η^2 (eta-square) is a measure of association showing the proportion of variance in life satisfaction scores explained by marital status.

Source: Catherine A. Faver, "Life Satisfaction and the Life-Cycle: The Effects of Values and Roles on Women's Well-Being, Sociology and Social Research 66 (July 1982) 435–451, Table 2. Copyright 1982 by the University of Southern California Press. Reprinted by permission.

basic family roles. What is more interesting, however, is that the effect of marital status on satisfaction is even stronger for those with low career values than for those with high family values. This suggests that career interest is an important mediator of the relationship between marital status and life satisfaction. For many women, a career provides an alternative arena of involvement and source of gratification. If a woman does not develop a career, however, she is more likely to put all her eggs in the basket of family roles, and marriage is thus more crucial to satisfaction. Conversely, interest in a career seems to reduce the importance of marriage to women's satisfaction.

These findings do not deny the importance of marital status as a determinant of women's life satisfaction. Yet they do suggest that career involvement reduces the significance of marriage to women's happiness. Or, to put it another way, marriage has a significant impact on satisfaction primarily among those who have not developed career interests. Thus, although relatively few in number in our particular sample, it is the single women without strong career investment who are in the most disadvantaged, vulnerable position.

Employment status also has a significant effect on satisfaction. Women who are employed full-time are most satisfied with their lives, followed by part-time workers and the nonemployed. Yet, this positive relationship between employment and satisfaction is significant among those with high, but not low, career values. This suggests that paid employment is a decisive factor in overall satisfaction primarily among women who regard their work outside the home as an important arena of involvement and achievement.

In examining the relationship between employment and satisfaction, it is important to distinguish further between married and single women. Because single women generally must work outside the home, we find less variation in their employment status. Thus, there is less likely to be a discernible association between employment and satisfaction. Indeed, much of the research on women's employment has focused on married women, who are more likely to have some degree of choice about whether and when to seek employment.

In our sample, only about 15.5 percent of the single women are not employed. Thus, not surprisingly, the relationship between employment and satisfaction is irregular, and is not statistically significant among single women with either high or low career values. Among married women, however, there is a positive relationship between employment and satisfaction, and this relationship is statistically significant and particularly strong among those with high career values (Table 3.4). Thus, for wives who regard a career as an important area for personal achievement, periods out of the labor force exact a significant cost in life satisfaction.

Our findings regarding the interacting effects of employment status and personal values on life satisfaction help to expand prior research. In an analysis of national survey data collected in 1971 and 1978, Campbell (1980) found that while the number of employed wives increased during this period, there were no significant differences in the psychological well-being of employed wives and homemakers in either year. Among wives who were college graduates, the pattern was slightly different. In 1971, psychological well-being favored the employed college graduate wives, but the 1978 data showed no differences in the two groups: "Married college graduate women who work are no more or less positive about their life or their marriage than those who stay home" (Campbell 1980:300). Campbell explains these findings by emphasizing the process of self-selection in woman's labor force participation: " . . . many or most married women have a realistic choice between being a homemaker and taking a job . . . . For the most part these women seem to be sorting themselves into the roles they prefer at that stage of their lives" (1980:301). In support of this assertion, Campbell reports that in the 1978 survey, about 80 percent of the married homemakers and 75 percent of the employed wives indicated a preference for their respective, current roles.

But in further analysis, Campbell (1980) shows that dissatisfaction results when there is a discrepancy between a woman's preferred and enacted roles. Distinguishing unemployed women--those who desired employment but were currently not employed--from employed wives and married homemakers, he found that the unemployed women were the least satisfied of the three groups. Many of the unemployed women were also separated or divorced, and were undoubtedly coping with multiple problems. Thus, Campbell's

Table 3.4. One-Way ANOVA of Life Satisfaction by Employment Status, by Career Values: Married Respondents Only

Employment Status	Mean Life Satisfaction Score	N	F-Statistic	Probability	η^2 [*]
		High Career Values			
Not employed	3.65	95	28.49	< .0001	.1085
Employed part-time	4.08	144			
Employed full-time	4.50	232			
		Low Career Values			
Not employed	3.98	127	2.44	.0893	.0158
Employed part-time	4.21	103			
Employed full-time	4.29	77			

[*] η^2 is a measure of association showing the proportion of variance in life satisfaction scores explained by employment status.

Source: Catherine A. Faver, "Life Satisfaction and the Life Cycle: The Effects of Values and Roles on Women's Well-Being," Sociology and Social Research 66 (July 1982): 435–451, Table 3. Copyright 1982 by the University of Southern California Press. Adapted by permission.

51

findings seem to emphasize the importance of objective life situation, in conjunction with personal preferences, in determining a person's sense of well-being.

Campbell's (1980) findings support our basic hypothesis that life satisfaction depends on the degree of congruence between an individual's values and roles. And he goes further, arguing that today, most women are exercising choice in adopting the roles they prefer at various stages in their lives. Nevertheless, Laws (1978) suggests that in the study of women and employment, it is fallacious to assume that choice is always operative. Indeed, women in particular subgroups, and at particular life-cycle stages, are more likely to feel constrained in their choice of the extent and nature of their employment.

Earlier we noted that discrimination in the labor market and the constraints of family demands inhibit women's choice and advancement in professional careers (Fox & Hesse-Biber 1984: ch. 6). Despite the sharp increase in women's labor force participation, opportunities for women are still quite limited in the top positions. Thus, "the higher the rank, the fewer the women" is still true. Moreover, the nature of professional employment makes it particularly difficult to combine with homemaking. Professional employment requires extensive commitments of time and energy, and is frequently not confined to the eight-hour day. And the best jobs are rarely available on a part-time basis. Furthermore, the early, and often most demanding, career stages frequently coincide with the childbearing and early child-rearing period in the family life cycle. In sum, women who aspire to professional careers may have special difficulties in exercising choice and actualizing their preferences in employment (see also Fox & Hesse-Biber 1984). Since many of the women in our sample are highly educated and career-oriented, they are, as a group, especially vulnerable to these particular constraints.

In the sample as a whole, we have already found that discrepancies between women's values, or preferences, and their actual role opportunities in family and employment adversely affect life satisfaction. In subsequent chapters we will see that these discrepancies are especially likely to occur, and to lower satisfaction, among particular subgroups and at specific life-cycle stages.

SUMMARY

This chapter began to examine generational and life-cycle transitions in women's lives by comparing the attitudes and values of women in three age cohorts: 22-34, 35-44, and 45-64. We found that the proportion of women with high achievement orientation does not vary significantly among the three cohorts, suggesting stability in the level of women's achievement orientation across generations and life-cycle stages. Yet, there are significant age cohort differences in career orientation and attainment values, suggesting generational transitions in the expression of achievement orientation. Compared with older women, a higher proportion of younger women in the sample are career-oriented. Furthermore, young women are more likely to have high career and low family values, while older women are more likely to have low career and high family values. Nevertheless, slightly over a fourth of the women in each cohort have both high career and high family values. And the decline in family values is not as sharp as the increase in career values. These findings support prior studies suggesting that many young women are unwilling to substitute career for family; instead, they want both.

Several intercohort differences seem to reflect contrasting generational and life-cycle transitions. The relationship between achievement orientation and career orientation is stronger among younger women, suggesting a generational transition toward the channeling of achievement orientation into careers. At the same time, however, career orientation is most strongly related to career values in the oldest cohort, suggesting that women have more time to actualize their career plans during the later stages of the life cycle.

Although there are significant intercohort differences in career orientation and career values, actual rates of full-time employment vary little across the three age groups. And, despite the high educational level of the CEW women, their full-time employment rates differ little from those of women in a nationally representative sample. Yet, compared with the national sample, the CEW women within each cohort are about three times as likely to be employed part-time. Thus, whether by constraint or by choice, some career-oriented women seem to express their career interests through part-time employment.

Compared with achievement orientation, career and family values are much stronger predictors of employment status. A combination of career and family values best predicts employment status among women in the two younger cohorts, many of whom are in the childbearing and early child-rearing stages of the family life cycle. Yet, among women aged 45-64, who are likely to be in the child-launching or postparental stage, career values alone are the best predictors of employment. These findings suggest that women's labor force participation is partially a function of the interaction between career and family task demands and values.

In the sample as a whole, the effects of marital and employment statuses on well-being are partially dependent on value orientation. Thus, among respondents with high family values or low career values, married women are significantly more satisfied than single women. And, among married women with high career or low family values, employment is positively related to satisfaction. These findings suggest that satisfaction depends on the availability of opportunities to express individual values.

NOTES

1. The data from the Spring 1977 General Social Survey were made available by the Inter-University Consortium for Political and Social Research. The data for the Spring 1977 General Social Survey, National Data Program for the Social Sciences, were originally collected by James A. Davis of the National Opinion Research Center, University of Chicago, and were distributed by Roper Public Opinion Research Center, Williams College. Neither the original collector of the data nor the consortium bears any responsibility for the tabulations presented in this chapter.

2. Never-married, separated, divorced, and widowed women were included in one category in this analysis because research indicates that married women are happier than all groups of single women. Furthermore, in analysis not reported here, we found no significant differences in the life satisfaction of three categories of single women: never-married, separated/divorced, and widowed.

4.

AGES 22-34: THE PREFAMILY AND EARLY FAMILY STAGE

During early adulthood, women move through several important stages and transitions in the individual and family life cycle. Thus, the five life-cycle groups within this age cohort of our sample represent a diversity of positions in the social structure (see Table 4.1).

Of the single, childless women, about 80 percent have never married, and the remaining 20 percent are separated or divorced.   Although most are likely to marry or remarry, some may not. In fact, recent statistics show an increase in the proportion of young women who are single. Some young women may be hesitant to marry because of the high divorce rate, while others may simply perceive alternatives to marriage (Gluck et al. 1980).

Nevertheless, for most single young women the early adult years, including the prefamily stage, are a difficult period. For some, the desire to marry creates ambivalence about career preparation (Angrist & Almquist 1975). Other young women actively decide to delay marriage for the sake of their careers. These women generally have little societal or familial support for their nontraditional goals, and many confront active discrimination from the traditionally male occupational world (Bernard 1975; Rossi 1966; Disch 1977).

Table 4.1. Ages 22–34: Marital Status and Age of Youngest Child, by Life-Cycle Group

Group	Marital Status	N	Percent	Age of Youngest Child	N	Percent	Group N	Percent of Total Cohort
(1)	Single, childless women (Sing, none)						91	23.95
	Never married	73	80.22					
	Separated/divorced	18	19.78					
Total		91	100.00					
(2)	Married, childless women (Mar, none)						68	17.89
	Married	68	100.00					
(3)	Married mother of pre-school children (Mar, presc)						132	34.74
	Married	132	100.00	1–5	132	100.00		
(4)	Married mothers of elementary school children (Mar, elem)						55	14.47
	Married	55	100.00	6–12	55	100.00		
(5)	Single mothers (Sing, chil)						34	8.95
	Never married	3	8.82	1–5	11	32.35		
	Separated/divorced	31	91.18	6–12	22	64.71		
				13–18	1	2.94		
Total		34	100.00		34	100.00		
Grand total							380	100.00

Note: The abbreviations in parentheses will be used in subsequent tables in this chapter.
Source: Prepared by author.

56

Moreover, young career women often lack role models or mentors (Fox & Hesse-Biber 1984, ch. 6; Gluck et al. 1980).

If a woman does not marry before her late twenties or early thirties, her likelihood of marrying decreases as the pool of eligible men diminishes. On a personal and emotional level, the young woman must reconcile herself to this possibility. At the same time, she may begin to give her career more serious consideration (Gluck et al. 1980). However, the exact developmental sequence involved in marriage and career for women is unclear and variable. Some young women remain single in order to pursue a career, while others increase their career commitment if they do not marry (Huston-Stein & Higgins-Trenk 1978).

With marriage, the single young woman moves into the first stage of the family life cycle, represented in our sample by the married childless women. Although the early years of marriage entail some adjustment, this stage is an extremely satisfying period for the wife (Cambell 1975). For some women, accomplishment in the traditionally feminine area of affiliation frees them psychologically to pursue achievement in other areas (Bardwick 1971). Currently, relatively few women drop out of the labor force when they marry, and many actively pursue careers until the birth of their first child. Although women have the major responsibility for household tasks at this stage, as in the later stages, the marriage is likely to be relatively more egalitarian during this early period when the wife is employed (Gluck et al. 1980).

For many women, the decision whether to have children is very difficult (Fabe & Wikler 1979). In fact, there are at least three subgroups of childless women: the involuntarily childless, the postponers, and the voluntarily childless (Houseknecht 1979). Recent statistics reflect a rise both in childlessness and in the intention to remain childless (Blake 1979). For example, in 1976, 17 percent of the single women aged 18 to 24 reported that they expected to remain childless (U.S. Department of Commerce, Bureau of the Census 1977:28, cited in Blake 1979). The "postponers" include those who "drift" into childlessness through extended delay (Gluck et al. 1980). A wife's increasing involvement with her career and unwillingness to forgo her income have been cited as factors in the drift into childlessness (Bernard 1974).

With the birth of her first child, a woman moves into early motherhood, represented by our third life-cycle group. Much has been written about the difficulties of this period. While the transition to motherhood may not represent a true "crisis" (Mikus 1980), this transition and the subsequent preschool family stage are often quite stressful (Mikus 1980; Rossi 1968; Bernard 1974). Nevertheless, some women do find fulfillment through creative child rearing during early motherhood.

Regardless of the level of stress, the transition to motherhood does involve some important changes. Labor force participation drops abruptly during this period, as employed wives leave the labor force to care for their infants (Taeuber & Sweet 1976). If a woman drops out of the labor force, she must adjust to the loss of her work role, and she may feel a need to justify her decision (Gluck et al. 1980), perhaps especially to other young career women. On the other hand, the woman who continues to work outside the home during the preschool family stage must deal with many of the practical problems and issues of managing multiple (family and work) roles (Gluck et al. 1980).

When her youngest child starts school, a woman moves into the period of middle motherhood, represented in this cohort by the mothers of elementary school children in our fourth life-cycle group. A woman who has remained at home during the preschool family stage is now freed from the responsibility of constant child care. With liberation, however, come choice and the stress of decision making. She can go back to school, take a job or begin a career, increase her volunteer activities, or continue to focus on the homemaker and mother roles. With each alternative there are costs and benefits (Bernard 1974, 1975). A woman who was employed during early motherhood may now change fields, pursue more training, set new goals, or increase her career commitment. For many women, the transition to middle motherhood affords the opportunity for reflection and change.

Among recent cohorts, the percentage of divorces occurring at early ages has increased (Huston-Stein & Higgins-Trenk 1978:272). Thus, as a result of the rising divorce rate, the mother-child family, represented by the single mothers in our fifth life-cycle group, is increasingly common.

A number of studies suggest that divorced women tend to be more career-oriented than their married counterparts (see, e.g., Feldman 1973; U.S. Department of Labor, Women's Bureau 1966). Again, however, the developmental sequence is unclear. For some women, interest in pursuing a career may be a disruptive factor in the marriage, while others become career-committed following divorce, in the process of working to support themselves and their children (see Huston-Stein & Higgins-Trenk 1978).

But regardless of their level of career commitment, the unique constraints, options, and pressures of single mothers powerfully shape their life patterns. For example, compared with that of married mothers, single mothers' labor force participation is affected more by economic necessity and less by their children's developmental stages. As a result, single mothers have higher employment rates in all categories of children's age (Taeuber & Sweet 1976; U.S. Department of Commerce, Bureau of the Census 1980). In our sample, it will be instructive to observe how the single mothers reflect the unique intertwining of work and family roles necessitated by their marital and parental status.

These five life-cycle groups thus represent distinctly different positions in the social structure and different stages in the individual and family life cycle. Having sketched briefly some of the opportunities and constraints associated with each position, we can now consider related differences in both attitudes and behavior.

ACHIEVEMENT ORIENTATION

Our earlier analysis revealed similarity in achievement orientation among women of different age cohorts. It is possible, however, that variations in achievement orientation are associated with changes in marital and parental status, as women move through the family life cycle. Baruch (1967) posited a temporal cycle in achievement motivation related to both age and family situation. In her sample of married women, she found that achievement motivation was highest during the prechildren stage, among women just five years out of college. The dip in achievement motivation, occurring among women ten years past college graduation, coincided with the period of family expansion. When the family was fully established, at 15 years past college, achievement motivation again rose.

We maintain, however, that achievement orientation remains stable, while the way it is expressed changes, with variations in family life-cycle stage. The division of this cohort into life-cycle groups enables us to test further the hypothesis of stability in achievement orientation across the life cycle.

Table 4.2 indicates that the relationship between achievement orientation and life-cycle group does not quite reach the conventional (.05) level of statistical significance. The question, then, is whether the differences that exist are theoretically meaningful. If, for comparative purposes, we consider only the three groups of married women, there is some similarity with Baruch's findings. Achievement orientation is highest among married childless women, who are in the prechildren stage, and lowest among the mothers of preschoolers. The 3.3 percentage point difference in the level of achievement orientation of mothers of preschoolers and of elementary school children does not suggest, however, a sharp recovery of achievement orientation after the family is fully established. Single mothers, two-thirds of whom have children already in elementary school, have the lowest achievement orientation of all five groups. Thus far, then, our analysis does not reveal systematic changes in achievement orientation associated with movement through the family life cycle. Furthermore, to the extent that structural position shapes attitude, our data suggest that these life-cycle positions do not differ significantly in availability of reinforcement for the attitudes that constitute achievement orientation.

We must remember, however, that because of differences in our sample, these comparisons with Baruch's findings are rough. She selected women who are 5, 10, 15, 20, and 25 years past college graduation, so that women who were in different life-cycle stages were also in different age groups. In contrast, there is only a 12-year age range within the youngest cohort of our CEW sample, and the average age of the women in the five life-cycle groups varies little. This means that while Baruch was simultaneously comparing women of different ages and life-cycle stages, here we are comparing women who are in different life-cycle stages but similar in age. Nevertheless, our findings do not suggest marked changes in achievement orientation with transitions in family life-cycle stage, at least among the young women in this relatively narrow age range.

Table. 4.2. Ages 22-34: Achievement Orientation, Career Orientation, Career Values, Family Values, and Full-time Employment, by Life-Cycle Group

Life-Cycle Group	High Achievement Orientation (percent)	Career-Oriented (percent)	High Career Values (percent)	High Family Values (percent)	Employed Full-Time (percent)
Sing, none	64.8	92.9	94.3	15.9	66.3
Mar, none	76.9	96.9	90.8	23.4	62.7
Mar, presc	57.8	90.1	59.2	71.7	13.8
Mar, elem	61.1	96.1	82.4	54.7	47.2
Sing, chil	51.5	93.8	81.8	39.4	55.9
	$\chi^2 (4) = 8.92^*$	$\chi^2 (4) = 3.98$	$\chi^2 (4) = 48.07^{**}$	$\chi^2 (4) = 79.11^{**}$	$\chi^2 (8) = 82.61^{**}$

Note: The χ^2 statistics test the significance of the association between life-cycle group and each variable.

   * $p = .06.$
  ** $p < .0001.$
Source: Prepared by author.

CAREER ORIENTATION

should be Laura

In the youngest cohort, at least 90 percent of the women in each life-cycle group are career-oriented; that is, they think of themselves as having or planning a career (Table 4.2). Among women of such diverse marital and parental statuses, the low variance in career orientation is particularly notable, emphasizing the rising career aspirations of young women. Although the data are cross-sectional, they suggest that young women maintain a strong interest in career achievement throughout the periods of family formation and expansion. In other words, this pattern suggests that movement into the family life cycle does not significantly alter a young woman's plans to pursue a career. Indeed, at least the intention to pursue a career remains strong, even during the demanding stage of family expansion.

Considered with prior studies of women's career orientation, our findings suggest an important generational change. We know that studies of successive cohorts of young women reveal marked increases in career orientation--that is, in the intention to pursue a career (Cross 1975; Helson 1975; Parelius 1975). In general, these studies show an increasing proportion of young women who want to combine marriage, children, and career (see, e.g., Cross 1975; Parelius 1975).

Prior research suggests, moreover, that young women's career intentions have often been deflected during the family building and early child-rearing years. And for some young women, even the intention to pursue a career may not have developed as long as marriage and child rearing were anticipated. Serious career interest may have developed if a woman remained single; or if she did marry, career interest may have developed or reemerged once the children were in school. In short, at least for earlier generations of women, career orientation tended to reflect a developmental pattern related to such major life events as marriage, childbearing and child rearing, and divorce (see Huston-Stein & Higgins-Trenk 1978).

To some extent, this pattern may still hold true. Nevertheless, our data suggest that, at least for some women in recent cohorts, career intentions are not entirely deflected by family roles and responsibilities. Indeed, intentions to pursue a career remain strong even during the difficult and demanding period of family expansion.

Several studies illustrate the relationship between family roles and career orientation among earlier cohorts of women. In 1965, Harmon (1970) surveyed a group of women who had entered college in 1953-55. These women would be in the same age bracket as our middle (35-44) cohort. In this study, Harmon found no relationship between career commitment (committed vs. noncommitted) in 1965 and the women's recollections of their employment plans at age 18. The women's life patterns, however, did distinguish the career committed from the noncommitted. "The career committed group attended college longer, worked more years after leaving college, married later in life, bore fewer children before 1965, and bore them at more advanced ages than the noncommitted group did" (Harmon 1970:77). Moreover, compared with the noncommitted group, the career committed group included more unmarried women.

A seven-year longitudinal follow-up study assessed change and stability in career plans, and examined the family status and employment histories of almost 5,000 women college graduates of the class of 1957 (U.S. Department of Labor, Women's Bureau 1966). These women were about the same age as those in Harmon's (1970) study, and thus also would be in the same age range as our middle cohort. A comparison of the women's career plans in 1957 and 1964 revealed that of those who were interested in pursuing a career in 1957, 59 percent had that same intention in 1964, while only 5 percent of this group had no plan for employment in the future. On the other hand, of those who in 1957 had indicated no future employment plans, 41 percent still had no employment plans in 1964, while 9 percent of this group had become interested in having a career. Thus, the findings indicated some degree of both stability and change in young women's career orientation and employment plans.

Moreover, this study also indicated that the young women's career plans in 1964 were definitely related to their marital and parental status, suggesting the developmental pattern we noted earlier. Specifically, 63 percent of the never-married women, about 75 percent of the married women with children aged 6 to 17, and 75 percent of the widowed, separated, or divorced women wanted to have a career. Yet, only 30 percent of the married childless women, and 12 percent of the married mothers of preschool children intended to have a career (U.S. Department of Labor, Women's Bureau 1966). Although these are cross-sectional differences, the data do suggest that anticipation of marriage may temper career involvement among never-married young women. Then, when a young woman marries and is anticipating having children, or is rearing preschoolers, career orientation declines. Once past the early child-rearing years, however, interest in a career is renewed. Among the formerly married, career commitment is particularly high, whether that commitment precedes or follows the experience of marital dissolution. It is likely that among both single and married women, career commitment increases with increasing involvement in employment (Huston-Stein & Higgins-Trenk 1978).

Another, more recent follow-up study assessed stability and change in the career and family orientations of a slightly younger cohort of women (Almquist et al. 1980). The sample in this study was a group of 64 women, graduating in 1968, who had participated in a four-year longitudinal study during their college experience (see Angrist & Almquist 1975 for a discussion of the original study). These women would have been approximately age 31 in 1977 (the year of the present study), and thus would be in the same age range as the older members of our youngest cohort.

The Almquist (Almquist et al. 1980) follow up study, conducted in 1975, compared the women's aspirations as college seniors with their actual life-styles during the seven-year interim and with their current (1975) aspirations and plans. In terms of life-style patterns and future aspirations, the researchers distinguished three groups: careerists, "who have definite plans for specific careers"; familists, "who are mainly oriented toward rearing children, having leisure activities, and working only occasionally"; and workers, "who envision keeping their partial work commitments or returning to the labor force soon, but without a definite career" (Almquist et al. 1980:379). In a comparison of senior aspirations with current aspirations, the findings showed that among those who had been career-oriented as seniors, 51.6 percent were careerists, 29 percent were workers, and 19.4 percent were familists in their current aspirations. And, of those who had been family-oriented as seniors, 42.9 percent were careerists, 9.5 percent were workers, and 47.6 percent were familists in their current aspirations (percentages computed from Table 4 in Almquist et al. 1980). Thus, while there was a greater tendency to develop or maintain a career or work orientation than a family orientation, there was still a great deal of alteration in aspirations during early adulthood in this young cohort.

To summarize, studies of successive cohorts have revealed increasing career orientation among women in college (Cross 1975; Parelius 1975). At the same time, however, studies of earlier cohorts suggest that women's career orientation changes, and often declines, during early adulthood, as they move through the early stages of the family life cycle. And even the Almquist study (Almquist et al. 1980) of a fairly recent cohort suggests much instability in career orientation during the first seven years after college graduation.

Yet, in the present study we found a high proportion of career-oriented women in each life-cycle group in our youngest cohort (Table 4.2). In contrast with earlier studies, our findings thus suggest that young women's career plans are not sharply determined or altered by marital status and family roles. Instead, young women maintain an intention to pursue a career throughout the early adult, family formation and family expansion years. If this pattern is true for a more general population of college-educated women, then it may represent an important generational transition in women's plans and aspirations.

This interpretation, however, must be tempered by several considerations. Without longitudinal data, we cannot say definitively that our findings represent a pattern of developmental stability in career orientation across life-cycle stages. Nor can we assess stability and change in career orientation from college age (18-22) through early adulthood. Among the women in our sample, intention to pursue a career may represent a recent development, rather than the maintenance of earlier career interest. Moreover, the high proportion of career-oriented women in each life-cycle group may reflect the selective nature of the sample, since all of the women had contacted a university's Center for Continuing Education of Women. Nevertheless, our findings suggest an important generational change, and warrant further investigation in larger, more representative samples of current cohorts of young women.

ATTAINMENT VALUES

Thus far, our results suggest that both achievement orientation and career orientation are relatively stable as women move through various stages of the individual and family life cycle. Strong shifts may nevertheless occur in the expression of achievement and career orientation.

Before they have children, women often channel their achievement orientation into career development. Then, during the period of family expansion, some highly educated women gratify their achievement needs through creative child rearing (Veroff & Feld 1970; Bardwick 1971). When the children reach school age, women are released from many child-care responsibilities and also have fewer opportunities to engage in some of the creative aspects of mothering. As a result, they may redirect their achievement orientation into beginning or resuming a career. While the intention to pursue a career (that is, career orientation) may have been present during the preschool family years, the opportunities to do so may have been limited. Changes in the expression of achievement orientation thus correspond to changes in the demands of family roles. This pattern suggests a temporal cycle in the expression, rather than the level, of women's achievement orientation. While a woman's family status does not significantly alter her level of achievement orientation, it powerfully affects the way it is expressed.

As we have seen, in this cohort there is wide diversity in life-cycle stage, yet little variance in career orientation. Thus, the effect of family status on the channeling of achievement orientation into career or family attainment should be clearly evident, uncontaminated by generational differences in the basic desire to pursue a career.

In fact, in accordance with the high proportion of career-oriented women in this cohort, our analysis reveals an overall pattern of high career values across life-cycle groups (Table 4.2). Notably, however, only 59 percent of the married mothers of preschoolers, compared with at least 81 percent of the women in each of the other groups, have high career values.

Moreover, the shifts in career values that occur coincide with major changes in family responsibilities. Single and married childless women, in the premarriage and prechildren stages, have the highest career values. Then, as we have noted, a sharp drop occurs during the preschool family stage, when family demands are strongest. After the children are in school, career values rise abruptly, reflecting a rechanneling of achievement orientation. Single mothers, who often provide the sole support for their children, have understandably high career values, although a third of these women have preschool children. Thus, although virtually all the women in this cohort regard themselves as having or planning a career, the importance they currently assign to career attainment is significantly affected by marital and parental status.

There is greater variance among life-cycle groups in family than in career values (Table 4.2). Family values are lowest among single, childless women, rise slightly with marriage, and soar during the period of family expansion. Indeed, mothers of preschoolers are three times as likely as married childless women to have high family values. Clearly, during early motherhood, child rearing becomes an area of central interest and achievement concern. Although family values drop when all the children are in school, they nevertheless remain higher than in the prechildren stages. Single mothers have lower family values than either group of married mothers, perhaps reflecting their need to emphasize the breadwinner rather than the traditional maternal role.

Comparision of career and family values reveals the relative effects of marital and parental status, and further emphasizes critical transition points in the family life cycle. We see that motherhood has a greater impact than marriage on attainment values. Compared with single, childless women, only a slightly smaller proportion of married childless women have high career values, and a slightly larger proportion have high family values (Table 4.2).

Yet, among married women, two critical shifts in attainment values coincide with changes in maternal status. First, the transition from childlessness to early motherhood marks the greatest change in attainment values. In this transition, family values increase much more than career values decline (Table 4.2). And, considering the combination of career and family values, the proportion of women emphasizing career over family drops over 50 percentage points, while the proportion emphasizing family over career increases almost 30 percentage points in this transition (Table 4.3). Although many single mothers have preschool children, their emphasis on career over family may be attributed to the economic responsibilities of single parenthood (Table 4.3).

Thus far, these comparisons emphasize the importance of the transition to motherhood, indicating the powerful effect of the maternal role on the channeling of achievement orientation. In this way, our findings are consistent with several recent studies (Daniels & Weingarten 1982; Schwartz 1980) that suggest that the maternal role takes precedence over the work role during early motherhood, even among career-oriented professional women. Nevertheless, the results of the present study also reflect a maintenance of relatively high interest in career attainment, even during the demanding preschool family stage.

Furthermore, our findings suggest that young women are determined to return to career attainment in middle motherhood, without relinquishing family values. The second important change in attainment values for married women is the transition from early to middle motherhood. In this shift, the increase in career values is slightly greater than the decline in family values (Table 4.2). Notably, only 17.5 percent of the mothers of preschoolers, compared with 44 percent of the mothers of elementary school children, have high career and low family values (Table 4.3). Moreover, the percentage with low career and high family values decreases by almost half in the transition to middle motherhood (Table 4.3). These figures thus suggest a sharp change in the channeling of women's achievement orientation when all the children are in school. Nevertheless, about two-fifths of each group of married mothers have both high career and high family values (Table 4.3).

Recently, adolescent girls and college women have expressed increasingly less willingness to focus their lives exclusively on the homemaker and mother roles. At the same time, however, they are not willing to forgo marriage and motherhood for the sake of a career (Bernard 1975; Cross 1975; Parelius 1975). Bernard (1975:91) offered the following summary of these changes:

> Young women rarely ask the old marriage-versus-career question now. More and more they ask instead, what else am I going to do besides being a mother? They take the "else" for granted.

Table 4.3. Ages 22-34: Combined Career and Family Values, by Life-Cycle Group (percentage distribution)

Life-Cycle Group	High Career High Family (percent)	High Career Low Family (percent)	Low Career High Family (percent)	Low Career Low Family (percent)	Total Percent	N
Sing, none	13.4	81.8	2.4	2.4	100.00	82
Mar, none	22.2	69.9	1.6	6.3	100.00	63
Mar, presc	40.5	17.5	31.0	11.0	100.00	126
Mar, elem	38.0	44.0	16.0	2.0	100.00	50
Sing, chil	27.3	54.5	12.1	6.1	100.00	33

χ^2 (12) = 109.37.
p < .0001.
Source: Prepared by author.

The present study shows how these plans are being actualized by adult women confronting the reality of their options and constraints. Here we find that young mothers are still very concerned with the maternal role. Family involvement is a central concern, especially when the children are young. Indeed, relatively few of the married mothers in this cohort emphasize career attainment over family interests during early motherhood, and almost a third place family over career. Yet, what is most notable is that even during the most demanding stage of motherhood, the mothers of preschoolers are just as likely as the mothers of school-age children to assign high importance to achievement in the areas of both career and family.

These findings suggest that young women do not abandon their career dreams when they become mothers. Earlier we saw that the mothers of preschoolers are just as career-oriented as the women in other life-cycle stages. Now we see that these young mothers not only think of themselves as having or planning careers, but also place high value on career attainment. A question that remains is to what extent they are currently involved in actualizing their career plans. To answer that question, it is now necessary to examine the employment behavior of the women in this cohort.

EMPLOYMENT STATUS

In recent years, some very striking and important changes in women's labor force participation have occurred among women aged 25 to 34. Fox and Hesse-Biber (1984:200) summarize these developments:

> Since 1970, the greatest increases in female labor force participation have been among women under age thirty-five and among mothers with preschool children (Kamerman and Kahn, 1981:25). By 1978, half of American mothers with children under age six, and 60 percent of the women in the prime childbearing and -caring years (ages twenty-five to twenty-nine) were working outside the home. These proportions are expected to be even larger in the next two decades--as each successive cohort of young women participates more fully in

the labor force (Lloyd and Niemi, 1979; Smith, 1979).

Despite these recent and anticipated gains, however, women's labor force participation is still tied to the family life cycle, with childbearing and child rearing exerting a significant influence on women's employment patterns (U.S. Department of Commerce, Bureau of the Census 1980:42). In 1978, married mothers of children under 3 years of age had a labor force participation rate of 37.6 percent, compared with a rate of 47.9 percent for those with children 3-5 (none under 3), and 57.2 percent for those with children 6-17. While single mothers have higher participation rates overall, the pattern is similar. Among divorced, widowed, and married/husband absent mothers, the comparable rates were 55.5 percent for those with children under 3, 63.9 percent for those with children 3-5, and 71.2 percent for those with children 6-17 (U.S. Department of Commerce, Bureau of the Census 1980: Table 6-6, p. 50).

At the time of the present study in the late 1970s, the employment status of the women in our youngest cohort reflected this intertwining of the family, social, and economic life-styles. Nearly two-thirds of the single childless women, over three-fifths of the married childless women, and well over half of the single mothers were employed full-time (Table 4.2). In sharp contrast is the extremely low full-time employment rate (13.8 percent) of the married mothers of preschool children. Yet, almost half of the married mothers of elementary school children are employed full-time (Table 4.2), suggesting a return to employment during middle motherhood.

The critical transitions to and from early motherhood are further reflected in the rates of nonemployment in this cohort. Although over a third (35.1 percent) of the married mothers of preschool children are employed part-time, slightly over half (51.1 percent) are not employed at all. This rate of nonemployment is about three times higher than that of married childless women (16.4 percent), and twice as high as that of the married mothers of elementary school children (24.5 percent).

Thus, despite uniformity in career orientation, the employment rates of women in this cohort are strongly related to marital and parental status, reflecting the incentives and constraints associated with different life-cycle stages. In sum, the data suggest the typical pattern: withdrawal from employment during the preschool family stage, and return to work when the children reach school age. In the next section, we will examine more carefully the discrepancies between young women's career-related attitudes and their actual employment status.

CAREER ORIENTATION, CAREER VALUES, AND EMPLOYMENT

Thus far we have considered separately career orientation, career values, and employment status in this cohort. Now we can refer to both prior research and our own findings to examine the relationships between career attitudes and actual employment behavior among women of different life-cycle stages.

Earlier we noted the strong relationship between family life-cycle stage and participation in the labor force, both in our own sample and in the general population of women. From this we may infer that childbearing and child rearing are major inhibitors of women's employment (see U.S. Department of Commerce, Bureau of the Census 1980:42). Women's own testimony confirms this inference. The seven-year follow-up study on the college class of 1957 (U.S. Department of Labor, Women's Bureau 1966) revealed that the birth and care of children was given as the main reason for leaving the labor force by 78 percent of married women with children under 6 years old, and by 37 percent of those whose youngest child was 6-17 years old.

Almquist's (Almquist et al. 1980) follow-up study of a college class of 1968, described earlier, not only found both stability and change in the women's career aspirations, but also revealed discrepancies between college plans and actual life-styles over the seven-year period. Of those who as seniors had been career-oriented (defined as a high willingness to work), 51.6 percent were careerists, 25.8 percent were workers, and 22.6 percent were familists in their life-style patterns over the seven years since graduation. Of those with a family orientation, or low desire to work, as seniors, 47.6 percent were careerists, 28.6 percent were workers, and 23.8 percent were familists in life-style pattern.

Despite these inconsistencies between college plans and life-style patterns, many of the women had been involved in employment to a greater extent than they had expected: "Whereas about 59 percent of seniors had expected to work, 72 percent of the alumnae were working at the time of the followup and only 5 percent had not worked at all since graduation" (Almquist et al. 1980:371). Most notably, in a comparison of senior and current attitudes toward working, the researchers found "Substantial change . . . toward favoring gainful employment even when children are young and the husband's salary is adequate" (Almquist et al. 1980:373). Interest in an actual career, however, was not as strong as the interest in employment. And for the women who had exhibited the "worker" life-style, family-related contingencies seemed especially important in determining extent of employment. To summarize, these findings suggest change over time in career and work attitudes; discrepancies between employment attitudes and involvement; and the importance of family roles and responsibilities in affecting both employment attitudes and involvement, and in mediating the relationship, over time, between career interest and employment status.

Parelius' (1975) study of college women in a slightly younger cohort also revealed an increasing willingness to work outside the home during the preschool family stage. This study compared the work plans and attitudes of students in a state-supported women's college in 1969 and 1973. As noted previously, the study revealed an increase in the percentage of women wanting to combine marriage, family, and career. Moreover, the data further suggested

> . . . that among those women intending to "combine marriage, family, and a career," there was a shift away from planning an "interrupted" career pattern and toward planning a "double track" pattern (Cooper, as cited in Bernard, 1971:165) of concurrent working and homemaking (Parelius 1975:425).

In other words, there was an increasing tendency to plan for simultaneous involvement in work and family roles, rather than role sequencing (see Voydanoff 1980).

The results of the present study suggest, however, that the goal of simultaneous work and family role involvement is often not met during the preschool family stage. We observed that despite uniformity in career orientation, or intention to pursue a career, employment rates are strongly related to marital and parental status. In fact, the married mothers of preschool children in this cohort are even less likely to be employed full-time than their counterparts in the general population. National labor statistics for 1977 (the year of the present study) revealed that 23 percent of married mothers, all of whose children were under six years of age, were employed full-time, compared with a full-time employment rate of only 13.8 percent for the married mothers of preschoolers in this cohort of our sample.(1) Furthermore, the extent to which both career orientation and career values exceed full-time employment--discrepancies of 76.4 and 45.5 percentage points, respectively--is greater in this group of young mothers than in the other life-cycle groups.

These findings suggest a pattern of deferral, rather than abandonment, of the intention to pursue a career during early motherhood. In addition, they suggest that young mothers continue to value career achievement during the preschool family stage. An important question, however, is to what extent this pattern of deferral represents choice--a voluntary channeling of achievement orientation into the family and other areas--or constraint--an imposition of family responsibilities and other structural barriers that limits women's employment, especially during early motherhood.

The reasons for deferring career plans undoubtedly vary widely among women, and for any particular woman, factors involving both choice and constraint may affect the employment decision. Indeed, a woman's employment status, especially during the early child-rearing years, may be affected by a number of complex, interrelated factors. Among the mothers of preschool children in our youngest cohort, the lower-than-average employment rate, and the discrepancy between career values and employment, may reflect the particular constraints and incentives likely to affect the type of women in our sample: highly educated, relatively affluent women who have contacted a university-affiliated center for continuing education of women. In fact, there are several plausible explanations for the observed patterns.

First, some of the women in this cohort were attending school at the time of the study. For some of them, employment activity may have been curtailed while completing undergraduate or graduate/professional training. In other words, the need for career preparation may partially explain the pattern of high career values and relatively low employment rates.

Second, the observed patterns may represent career deferral by choice. Given the high family values of many young mothers (Table 4.2), some may actively choose to delay full-time career pursuits in order to spend more time in the home during the early child-rearing years. Indeed, despite young women's increasing career orientation, the Parelius study of college women, cited above, found that in both 1969 and 1973 "only a small minority of ... women indicated that they would give up marriage or motherhood for career success"(1975:425). Thus, although national surveys show that work is becoming central in women's lives, and that many women would choose employment even in the absence of economic need (Kamerman & Kahn 1981:25, cited in Fox & Hesse-Biber 1984:200), family roles are still highly valued by many women, and this factor enters into the decision about whether to seek employment during the preschool family stage. In fact, upon becoming mothers, some professional women have been surprised at how much they enjoy their new baby and their new role. Having expected motherhood to interfere with their careers, some find instead that career responsibilities prevent them from taking full advantage of all the pleasurable experiences of motherhood (see Daniels & Weingarten 1982).

Nevertheless, even if a woman values family over career, this does not necessarily mean that she would automatically reject labor force participation altogether during the preschool family stage. There are other important considerations as well, many of which operate to constrain, or at least to inhibit, women's employment, despite high career values.

Primary among the constraints to women's employment are their traditional home and family responsibilities. Even when they are employed, women still bear the major responsibility for household management and child care (see Hofferth & Moore 1979; Meissner et al. 1975; Pleck 1981; Fox & Hesse-Biber 1984:179). Thus, rather than switching roles, employed women add a role:

> For the woman who is able to take on market
> work, the paid job is an additional occupation
> which, when combined with home work, means
> that she is pursuing a "dual" career (Kreps &
> Leaper 1976:69-70).

Furthermore, combining traditional maternal responsibilities with full-time professional employment is especially
difficult (Poloma 1972). A professional career requires
extensive commitments of time and energy, and simultaneous
demands from career and family can create difficult conflicts for women (see Fox & Hesse-Biber 1984:139-41). Moreover, current structural arrangements of American society,
including the lack of adequate child-care facilities, inflexible
work schedules, and the unavailability of good part-time jobs,
often exacerbate these conflicts (see Fox & Hesse-Biber
1984: chs. 8, 9). At the same time, however, a highly trained
woman may be reluctant to accept less than professional
employment, especially if a second income is not needed.

Many of the women in our sample are married to highly
educated, professional men, whose incomes may not necessitate a second source of support. As we noted earlier, many
women indicate a preference for employment even in the
absence of economic need (Kamerman & Kahn 1981:25, cited
in Fox & Hesse-Biber 1984). Nevertheless, when combined
with other relevant considerations, including the heavy child-
care tasks of early motherhood, a husband's high income may
be an important inhibitor of a woman's employment.

The nature of the husband's occupation, as well as his
income, may also decrease the likelihood of a wife's employment. The jobs of professional, high-income males often
entail a great deal of mobility, and their wives may be unable
to obtain appropriate employment in a new location (see Long
1974 and Miller 1966, both cited in Almquist et al. 1980).

Despite all these potential constraints and inhibitors of
women's employment, there is evidence that some women in
our sample may have worked out at least a partial solution to
the difficulties of combining employment with the responsibilities of early motherhood. Slightly over a third (35.1
percent) of the mothers of preschool children in this cohort
are employed part-time--a proportion greater than the part-
time employment rate of any other life-cycle group in this
cohort. Because of their higher-than-average educational

attainment, many of the CEW women may be able to obtain consulting, editing, college teaching, or other positions that allow flexibility in working hours, total working time, office location, and other employment conditions. They can thus maintain their professional involvement when family responsibilities, other obligations, or even personal preference preclude full-time employment. During early motherhood especially, part-time employment may be an important means of maintaining career involvement (see Schwartz 1980).

The data further suggest, however, that once the children reach school age, these young, highly educated, career-oriented women are eager to begin or resume full-time career activity. In this cohort, the full-time employment rate for married mothers of elementary school children is 47.2 percent, while national labor statistics for 1977 revealed a full-time employment rate of only 35 percent for married mothers of school-age children (6-17 years only).(2) Nevertheless, career orientation and career values still exceed the employment rate by 48.9 and 35.2 percentage points, respectively, even among these mothers of elementary school children in our youngest cohort. This suggests that the factors inhibiting the actualization of career plans during the preschool family stage continue to be operative during middle motherhood.

In this section we have considered a number of plausible explanations for the large discrepancies between career attitudes and employment status among many of the women in this cohort. In so doing, we raised the question of the extent to which these discrepancies represent constraint or choice. In comparing the relative life satisfaction of the life-cycle groups in this cohort, we can address this question further in the following section.

LIFE SATISFACTION

Previous research suggests that age and marital and parental status have an interactive effect on life satisfaction (Campbell 1975; Campbell et al. 1976). In fact, the variations in the life situations of the life-cycle groups defined in this cohort have been associated with extreme differences in life satisfaction.

Young single women are one of the most dissatisfied life-cycle groups (Campbell 1975). Marriage represents interpersonal "success" for women in American society; and because of occupational and economic discrimination, marriage may be the simplest route to financial support and security.(3) Thus, young women who are not married may feel like "multiple failures" (Disch 1977:1). Moreover, early adulthood can be a stressful period even for professional women, as they move through the difficult preparatory and launching stages of their careers (Rossi 1966).

Bernard (1981) noted that to the observer, young single women between roughly 18 and 26 years of age seem to be in "prime time." With the societal glorification of youth and beauty, they are primary models and targets for the production and marketing of numerous consumer goods, and it is upon this group of women that the male world bestows most of its romantic attention. Yet, to the young women themselves, this is frequently a difficult period, fraught with anxieties about relationships, careers, and the mixture and management of the two. National survey data reveal that young single women report markedly high stress and low satisfaction levels (Campbell 1975; Campbell et al. 1976).

In marked contrast with young single women, young married but childless women are characterized by low stress and high satisfaction levels (Campbell 1975; Campbell et al. 1976). In fact, Campbell (1975) found that young married women without children are one of the happiest of all life-cycle groups. They are enjoying the honeymoon stage of marriage, secure in having accomplished what is regarded as a central achievement for women.

Following the honeymoon stage for married women, life satisfaction drops sharply during the preschool family stage, then rises when all the children are in school (Campbell 1975). Earlier we referred to research on the stress of the early child-rearing years. Indeed, motherhood, like marriage, has traditionally been virtually nonoptional for women (Rossi 1966). As a result of socialization and societal pressure, many women feel that bearing and rearing children is an essential component of adult fulfillment. While these attitudes are changing, even modern young women often have difficulty determining whether the "need" they feel to have children arises from a true desire for the experiences of motherhood or from a deeply ingrained societal mandate (see Fabe & Wikler 1979).

At any rate, although women are trained to want and expect to be mothers, they are neither prepared for the realities of the role (Rossi 1968), nor given adequate familial and societal support to fulfill its demands (Bernard 1974). As a result, the transition to maternal status is often very difficult (Rossi 1968). In fact, Bernard (1974) argues that the structure of motherhood in American society fosters an "anxiety-guilt-fatigue" syndrome among mothers of young children. Relatively alone in an isolated household, the new mother must assume virtually full responsibility for a dependent and demanding infant. The personal testimonies of thousands of women, as well as official statistics regarding child abuse and the mental health of mothers, indicate that these conditions can be hazardous to both mothers and children. Indeed, in contrast with the highly satisfying honeymoon stage of early marriage, studies show that early motherhood is frequently marked by stress, dissatisfaction (Campbell 1975), and depression (Radloff 1975).

A number of studies have revealed low levels of satisfaction (Campbell 1975) and high levels of stress and psychiatric disorders among divorced and separated women (see, e.g., Berkman 1969; Briscoe et al. 1973; Chester 1971, cited in Tcheng-Laroche & Prince 1979). This is not surprising, considering the emotional pain of divorce (Herman 1977) and the heavy economic burdens and child-rearing responsibilities of many single mothers. Single mothers are often especially plagued by financial difficulties. American society, in emphasizing women's traditional family roles, has typically not prepared women for economic independence (Barnett & Baruch 1980). And for single mothers, discrimination stemming from societal, economic, and legal structures makes economic independence difficult to attain (Herman 1977). Thus, single mothers are likely to feel more constrained and to have fewer options than many other groups of women.

Yet, one recent study (Tcheng-Laroche & Prince 1979) suggests that adequate financial resources can make a critical difference in the adjustment and well-being of single mothers. It examined a nonprobability sample of 45 "economically viable, divorced or separated women with children" (Tcheng-Laroche & Prince 1979:36). Most of these well-educated, middle-income women, who were approximately 30 to 39 years old, were either working or attending school, and some were doing both. Interestingly, those who were employed experienced less stress than those not employed. And, overall, the women in the sample "enjoyed relatively good health and normal stress levels" (Tcheng-Laroche & Prince 1979:41-42). The results of the study thus showed that with adequate financial resources, these single mothers adjusted quite well to their role.

These findings suggest that with increasing career orientation, adjustment to divorce and establishment of economic independence may become less difficult for single mothers. Thus, in our sample it will be particularly interesting to compare the relative life satisfaction of young single mothers with high versus low career values.

This review of prior research suggests that the life-cycle groups in this cohort may be expected to differ significantly in life satisfaction, even without considering their career and family values. In general, our findings confirm this expectation. While the differences in mean life satisfaction scores are not large, they are statistically significant (F=3.20, p=.01) and are generally in the expected directions. Married, childless women are the most satisfied ($\bar{X}$=4.39); married mothers of preschoolers, the least satisfied ($\bar{X}$=3.89). Within this range, the mothers of elementary school children are relatively high ($\bar{X}$=4.22) and both single, childless women ($\bar{X}$=3.92) and single mothers ($\bar{X}$=4.06) are relatively low. Apparently the effects of marriage, divorce, and parenthood are generally the same in our more highly educated, relatively affluent sample as in the general population of women.

Each of the five life-cycle stages defined by marital and parental status in this cohort offers unique opportunities and constraints in regard to family and career involvement. In general, we expect life satisfaction to be affected not only by a woman's life-cycle position but also by the fit between her values and the opportunities she has to express them. Thus, when we further compare life satisfaction scores while controlling for career and family values, some important findings emerge.

First, our data support and expand earlier findings about the salience of marriage for women--particularly young women. Without controlling for career and family values, we found that married, childless women are the most satisfied, and single, childless women one of the two least satisfied life-cycle groups in this cohort. More important, when we include the women's values in the analysis, we find that single, childless women are the least satisfied of those with low career or high family values (Table 4.4). For these young woman, being unmarried blocks expression of high family values, or necessitates employment despite low career interest. Thus, dissatisfaction results from the discrepancy between their subjective expectations regarding marriage and family, and the economic demands and limitations of their single status.

Admittedly, in our relatively affluent, well-educated sample, there are few young single women with low career or high family values (Table 4.4). Although our sample thus reflects the rising career interest of young, college-educated women (Cross 1975), recent sex-role changes have had much less impact on the more family-centered young women of the lower classes (Lowenthal 1975). Hence, in a more representative sample, we might expect low career and high family values in a higher proportion of young single women --and, accordingly, higher rates of dissatisfaction.

In conjunction with prior studies, however, our findings suggest that the dissatisfaction of young single women could be somewhat alleviated by structural changes that reduce the discrepancies between women's values and role opportunities. Because of discrimination, women's objective job prospects and advancement opportunities are limited (Kanter 1977; Ratner 1980), and the lack of objective opportunities, in turn, can serve to depress aspiration levels (see Fox & Hesse-Biber 1984: chs. 3,6; Fox & Faver 1981; Kanter 1977). Essentially, then, because of limited alternatives and prospects in the occupational sphere, many young women turn to marriage as a source of both emotional gratification and financial security. Yet, prior research suggests that career aspirations rise to the level of available opportunities for advancement (Kanter 1977), and that economic independence reduces women's willingness to marry (see, e.g., Havens 1973).(4) Thus, societal changes aimed at expanding women's career opportunities may enhance career aspirations, reduce the pressure to marry, and thus raise satisfaction levels among young single women.

Our data also support prior studies showing early motherhood as a period of high stress and low satisfaction. We found that married mothers of preschool children are the least satisfied life-cycle group in the youngest cohort. More

Table 4.4. Ages 22-34: One-Way ANOVA of Life Satisfaction by Life-Cycle Group, by Career Values and Family Values

Life-Cycle Status	Mean Life Satisfaction Score	N	F-Statistic	Probability	η^2 *
		High Career Values			
Sing, none	3.94	83	3.03	.02	.0411
Mar, none	4.39	59			
Mar, presc	3.83	77			
Mar, elem	4.29	42			
Sing, chil	4.11	27			
		Low Career Values			
Sing, none	3.40	5	.69	.60	.0357
Mar, none	4.33	6			
Mar, presc	3.98	53			
Mar, elem	4.11	9			
Sing, chil	3.83	6			
		High Family Values			
Sing, none	3.46	13	2.84	.03	.0679
Mar, none	4.73	15			
Mar, presc	3.92	91			
Mar, elem	3.97	29			
Sing, chil	4.23	13			
		Low Family Values			
Sing, none	4.00	69	2.89	.02	.0564
Mar, none	4.27	49			
Mar, presc	3.72	36			
Mar, elem	4.54	24			
Sing, chil	3.95	20			

*η^2 is a measure of association showing the proportion of variance in life satisfaction scores explained by employment status.

Source: Catherine A. Faver, "Life Satisfaction and the Life Cycle: The Effects of Values and Roles on Women's Well-Being," Sociology and Social Research 66 (July 1982): 435-451, Table 51. Copyright 1982 by the University of Southern California Press. Reprinted by permission.

notably, these young mothers are especially dissatisfied if they have high career or low family values (Table 4.4). This suggests that high career orientation and low family interest are incompatible with the constraints and demands of early motherhood, as it is structured in American society.

As we saw earlier, our data suggest that the strong career interest of highly educated young women is maintained into adulthood, even during the demanding stage of early motherhood. Moreover, we found a sharp discrepancy between the level of career values and the rate of full-time employment among the young married mothers of preschool children in our sample. This discrepancy, together with our finding of low satisfaction among these young mothers, suggests that the pattern of withdrawal from the labor force during early motherhood reflects constraint, rather than choice, for many young women. Thus, if the trend of high career orientation among young women continues, and further extends to the less affluent, dissatisfaction may likewise become increasingly prevalent among homebound young mothers.

Structural changes that facilitate women's career participation and provide societal support for child rearing may reduce dissatisfaction among young mothers with high career values. This dual emphasis, on both expanding women's career opportunities and supporting the care and nurturing of children, is critical. As the "dual role hypothesis" (Gove & Tudor 1973; Radloff 1975) suggests, the individual with both family and employment roles has an alternative source of gratification when satisfactions from either of the two roles is low. Moreover, research suggests that during the preschool family stage, employment can provide a young mother with important gratifications that are unavailable at home (see Plunkett 1980).

At the same time, however, the addition of market work without reduction in traditional household and family responsibilities, especially during the preschool family stage, may serve to increase, rather than diminish, a young mother's distress (Gluck et al. 1980). As we noted earlier, "when women become employed, they don't relinquish housework for market work; rather, they add one work role to the other" (Fox & Hesse-Biber 1984:65). And during the preschool family stage, when housekeeping and child-care tasks are particularly heavy, the management of dual work roles is likely to be especially difficult.

Some young mothers have found that part-time employment provides a workable solution to the difficulties of combining career interest with family responsibilities during early motherhood (see Schwartz 1980). But the limited availability of such jobs, and their various drawbacks, including the frequent lack of fringe benefits and promotion opportunities (Smith 1978 and Greenwald 1977, both cited in Fox & Hesse-Biber 1984:193), make this solution untenable for many women.

More generally, a number of strategies have been suggested for "dual worker families" (that is, families in which both husband and wife are employed) to manage the demands of home and employment (Fox and Hesse-Biber 1984:ch. 8). In describing and summarizing these strategies for resolving conflicts between home and employment roles, Fox and Hesse-Biber (1984: ch. 8) distinguish between "individual resolutions," in which individual couples adapt their lives and schedules to fit the current institutional structures, and "structural resolutions," which entail changes in some of the basic institutional structures of society. Individual resolutions include strategies of time management, flexibility in household task division and child care, the sharing of parenting, and various means of compartmentalizing work and family life (see Fox & Hesse-Biber 1984: ch. 8). Among the structural resolutions are proposals for the expansion of part-time employment opportunities and the adoption of policies supporting child care through various services and/or benefits to parents (Fox & Hesse-Biber 1984: chs. 8, 9).

While a complete enumeration and discussion of these strategies is beyond the scope of this chapter, Fox and Hesse-Biber's (1984:192) conclusion regarding the limitations of the individual solutions, and the need for structural change, is worthy of note:

> Individual resolutions have only gotten men and women so far, and to some extent they have stretched the fiber of the family too thin. Hence, we must go beyond individual solutions, and examine possibilities for structural change within the society itself.

Indeed, given the scope and importance of the issues involved, individual strategies are inadequate. Instead, structural changes are needed to facilitate satisfying combinations of work and family roles, and to support the best possible care and rearing of children.

Surely many of the difficulties of child rearing, as well as the specific problems that employed women have in managing both family and work roles, extend into middle motherhood. Nevertheless, in accordance with prior research (e.g., Campbell 1975), our findings suggest that women's life satisfaction rises when all the children reach school age. We found that the married mothers of preschool children were the least satisfied group in this cohort, while the married mothers of elementary school children ranked next to the highest in satisfaction. When we included the women's values in the analysis, we found that the married mothers of preschool children are particularly dissatisfied if they have high career or low family values (Table 4.4).

Further examination suggests that not only women's satisfaction during the preschool family stage, but also their response to the transition to middle motherhood, depends on the relative value they attach to family versus career achievement and concerns. Among women with low career or high family values (those who were relatively less dissatisfied during early motherhood), the married mothers of elementary school children have only slightly higher average life satisfaction scores than the married mothers of preschool children. But among women with high career or low family values (those who were relatively more dissatisfied during early motherhood), married mothers of elementary school children have, relatively speaking, much higher average life satisfaction scores than married mothers of preschool children. And among the married mothers of elementary school children, those with high career or low family values have higher average life satisfaction scores than those with low career or high family values (Table 4.4).

These findings suggest that in the transition to middle motherhood, the sharpest changes occur among women with high career (or especially) low family values. These women are the most dissatisfied during early motherhood because of the incompatibility between their values and the constraints of the preschool family stage. Thus, the transition to middle motherhood may signify a welcome liberation. Once the children are in school, there is relief from the constraints of constant child care, and often there is greater opportunity for full-time employment and serious career pursuit.

But for women with low career or high family values, the transition to middle motherhood may not be such a welcome or satisfying change. These women may miss the rewarding aspects of full-time mothering, and if they are not involved in a career or other major, meaningful pursuits, they may feel somewhat at loose ends. Thus, their adjustment to middle motherhood may be difficult and unsatisfying, especially at first.

This again suggests the importance for life satisfaction of involvement in multiple roles. For example, a woman who has been employed part-time during early motherhood may have a satisfying consistency in her work role and identity during the transition to middle motherhood. This is not to imply that a career or job is the only, or even the most desirable, type of involvement for every woman; each woman must determine for herself the most important and meaningful use of her time and abilities. Nevertheless, if women had greater career opportunities, more young women would be likely to develop their skills and abilities early in adulthood, even before marriage and motherhood. Then, with part-time employment opportunities and other supports, they could maintain their career involvement through the preschool family stage, or more easily resume their training or employment during middle motherhood.

Moreover, as an additional safeguard against the potential problems of this transition, educational and career counseling for young women should provide realistic information about the stages of motherhood and should encourage women, through a type of anticipatory socialization, to prepare for the varying demands and opportunities of critical transitions. Finally, for women who are currently experiencing difficulty in sorting out the options of middle motherhood, certain types of assistance and supports are needed. These include counseling services, expanded part-time employment opportunities, and the strengthening of university programs for the nontraditional student.

Overall, the single mothers in this cohort are the middle-ranking group in average life satisfaction. But, as we found for the other groups, the single mothers' life satisfaction also varies somewhat, depending on their values. Average life satisfaction scores are higher among single mothers with high career or high family values than among those with low career or low family values (Table 4.4). These findings make sense intuitively. Because a single mother is often primarily responsible for both nurturing her children emotionally and providing them with economic support, she is likely to be happier in her roles if she places high value on both family and career involvement.

Further, our findings help to specify the conditions that may ease the transition to single motherhood. As we noted earlier, prior literature has frequently focused on the peculiar stresses and difficulties of single mothers, and these very real problems certainly should not be underestimated. At the same time, however, our findings support the results of a study (Tcheng-Laroche & Prince 1979), described earlier, which suggested the importance of adequate economic provision in facilitating adjustment to single motherhood. In our sample, we may assume that it is the women with high career values who are most likely to enjoy active career pursuit. And, despite discrimination in the labor market, the single mother who is engaged in a career may be better able to meet the economic needs of her children, and thus be more satisfied with her life.

In this cohort, thus far we have examined the relationship between life-cycle stage, defined by marital and parental status, and life satisfaction. But we would also expect life satisfaction to be affected by employment status. In fact, in this cohort, as in the sample as a whole, the relationship between employment status and life satisfaction is positive and statistically significant among those with high ($F=10.62$, $p < .001$), but not low ($F=.74$, $p=.48$), career values.

Furthermore, marital status also affects the relationship between employment and satisfaction. Among single women, life satisfaction is not significantly related to employment status for those with either high ($F=2.03$, $p=.136$) or low ($F=.364$, $p=.706$) career values. In fact, there is little variance in the career values and employment status of the single women in this cohort: over four-fifths are employed, either part- or full-time, and only about 10 percent have low career values. Thus, these factors are not useful in explaining the life satisfaction of single women.

Again, however, as in the sample as a whole, employment is strongly and significantly related to satisfaction among married women with high ($F=13.51$, $p < .001$), but not low ($F=.821$, $p=.44$), career values. Thus, paid employment is important to satisfaction primarily among married women who are specifically concerned with career attainment. This finding supports the argument that life satisfaction is a function not only of individual values or role opportunities, but also of the fit between them.

SUMMARY

The women in this cohort represent a diversity of individual and family life-cycle stages, ranging from the prefamily stage to middle motherhood. Despite differences in life-cycle stages, however, virtually all of the women either have or plan to have a career. Level of achievement orientation, too, does not vary significantly across life-cycle groups.

Nevertheless, differences in the values assigned to career and family attainment and in labor force participation suggest that the expression of achievement orientation does vary with life-cycle stage. Family values, which peak during early motherhood, are strongly related to marital and parental status. In contrast, the value of career attainment is relatively high at all stages, despite a dip in early motherhood. Furthermore, married mothers tend to value attainment through both career and family. Marital status and parental status also significantly affect labor force participation, with nonemployment highest among the married mothers of preschoolers.

The individual's position in the social structure, or life-cycle stage, thus emerges as an important determinant of the expression of achievement orientation and of labor force participation. Indeed, marital status and parental status affect both the value assigned to career attainment and the extent to which career values are actualized through employment.

Structural position directly affects life satisfaction, with satisfaction highest among married childless and employed women. But career and family values also mediate the relationship between work and family statuses and life satisfaction. Thus, for example, single, childless women are the least satisfied of those with low career or high family values, and married mothers of preschoolers are the least satisfied of those with high career or low family values. Furthermore, the strongest relationship between employment and satisfaction is among married women with high career values. In general, these findings support our hypothesis that satisfaction is dependent on the degree of congruence between individual values and role opportunities.

NOTES

1. The national rate was computed from U.S. Department of Commerce, Bureau of the Census (1978): 405, Table 659. Differences in the life-cycle categories used in the national labor statistics and in our study render this comparison imprecise. We are comparing the national rate for married women of any age, all of whose children are under age 6, with the rate of the women in our sample who are ages 22-34 and whose youngest child is under 6 years old.

2. The national rate was computed from U.S. Department of Commerce, Bureau of the Census (1978):405, Table 659. Differences in life-cycle categories used in the national labor statistics and in our study render this comparison imprecise. We are comparing the national rate for married women of any age, all of whose children are ages 6-17, with the rate of the women in our sample who are ages 22-34 and whose youngest child is 6-12 years old.

3. The financial security attained through marriage is tenuous, however, because it may be lost upon death or divorce of the spouse.

4. Economic independence, high income, and strong commitment to the labor force are negatively related to marriage rates, and positively related to divorce rates, among women (Moore & Sawhill 1976:106). It is possible that marriage and divorce rates are partial causes, rather than effects, in these associations (see Moore & Sawhill 1976:106, for alternative interpretations of these correlations). Nevertheless, it is equally plausible that economic independence reduces women's willingness to marry, as Havens (1973) suggests.

5.

AGES 35-44:
THE MIDFAMILY STAGE

The period around age 35 is a critical point for women (Bardwick 1980; Bernard 1981), a "crossroads" (Sheehy 1974: 261) at which they confront certain key issues and are likely to make important life changes. Reproductive capacities decline, and childless women, particularly, must begin to make some final decisions about childbearing (Bardwick 1980). For mothers, the last child is generally in school by this time, and many women enter or reenter the labor force, or return to school (Bardwick 1980; Bernard 1981; Sheehy 1974). Divorced women often remarry (Sheehy 1974). By age 35, many women have gained a degree of independence from both their husbands and their own mothers (Bernard 1981), and a career woman frequently gains independence from her mentor during her mid-to-late thirties (Sheehy 1974). In short, this stage is marked by numerous changes. While society generally views women in their late teens and early twenties as being in "prime time" (Bernard 1981), from the woman's perspective, prime time may begin as the nest empties and she gains new freedom and independence (Bernard, 1981).

In the present study, the 35-44 cohort is an important group reflecting and illustrating both life-cycle and generational transitions. To begin with, the three groups of married mothers represent three life-cycle stages: the mothers of preschool children represent early motherhood; the mothers of elementary school children represent the first phase of middle motherhood; and the mothers of adolescent and college-age youth represent the transition from middle to late motherhood (Table 5.1).

With respect to family life-cycle stage, the mothers of preschool children and the mothers of elementary school children have counterparts in the 22-34 cohort. Yet, the two groups differ from their younger counterparts in the timing of marriage and parenthood. And these differences in the timing of life-course events have potentially important consequences for career and family patterns, and overall life satisfaction. There are both costs and benefits in delaying the transition to motherhood. While delayed childbearing affords women the opportunity to become established in a career during their early twenties (Gluck et al. 1980), the late childbearers may have more difficulty adjusting to parenthood (Daniels & Weingarten 1982). The older mother has less energy than her younger counterpart, she may have difficulty balancing family responsibilities with a demanding career, and she may have little in common with other mothers her age, who are likely to have adolescent children (Gluck et al. 1980). Nevertheless, many older mothers find that they enjoy motherhood more than they had anticipated (Daniels & Weingarten 1982), and the benefits of delayed childbearing frequently outweigh the costs, particularly if a woman's career allows flexibility in her work schedule (Gluck et al. 1980).

But this cohort also includes a new group of married mothers, those whose youngest child is an adolescent or college-age youth. Compared with the other married mothers in this cohort, the mothers of adolescents are, on the average, slightly older, and they married and began childbearing at an earlier age. This late phase of middle motherhood has some unique strains, because both parent and child are in potentially difficult transition stages. While the mother is confronting the transition to middle age, and a decline in the motherhood function, the adolescent is struggling toward independence and adulthood, with a shift in allegiance from family to peers (Gluck et al. 1980).

Table 5.1. Ages 35–44: Marital Status and Age of Youngest Child, by Life-Cycle Group

Group	Marital Status	N	Percent	Age of Youngest Child	N	Percent	Group N	Percent of Total Cohort
(1)	Married mothers of preschool children (Mar, presc)						33	8.99
	Married	33	100.00	1–5	33	100.00		
(2)	Married mothers of elementary school children (Mar, elem)						160	43.60
	Married	160	100.00	6–12	160	100.00		
(3)	Married mothers of adolescent and young adult children (Mar, youth)						78	21.25
	Married	78	100.00	13–18	74	94.87		
				19–22	4	5.13		
Total		78	100.00		78	100.00		
(4)	Single mothers (Sing, chil)						56	15.26
	Separated/divorced	54	96.43	1–5	1	1.79		
	Widowed	2	3.57	6–12	24	42.85		
				13–18	30	53.57		
				19–22	1	1.79		
Total		56	100.00		56	100.00		
(5)	Childless women (Childless)						40	10.90
	Married	16	40.00					
	Never married	15	37.50					
	Separated/divorced	9	22.50					
Total		40	100.00					
Grand total							367	100.00

Note: The abbreviations in parentheses will be used in subsequent tables in this chapter.
Source: Prepared by author.

93

In the three groups of married mothers, age of youngest child is positively related to the average age of the mothers. In other words, the mothers of preschool children are, on the average, the youngest married mothers in this cohort, while the mothers of adolescents and college-age youth are the oldest. As we shall see, these age differences are reflected in differences in career and family attitudes in these three groups. The youngest mothers tend to resemble the women in the 22-34 cohort in attitudes and behavior, while the oldest mothers resemble women in the 45-64 cohort. The middle group--the mothers of elementary school children--fall somewhere between the other two groups, reflecting a combination of the two more distinctive generations. Thus, these three groups of married mothers reflect and illustrate the transition from one generation to another.

As in the 22-34 cohort, the 35-44 cohort includes a group of single mothers and a group of childless women (Table 5.1). However, these two groups differ in significant ways from their younger counterparts. The single mothers in the youngest cohort represented primarily early motherhood and the first phase of middle motherhood, while the 35-44-year-old single mothers span the entire stage of middle motherhood. Furthermore, while many of the 22-34-year-old childless women are perhaps anticipating motherhood in the future, the childless women in the 35-44 cohort are more likely to remain childless. These important differences between the single mothers and childless women in the two cohorts may be reflected in differences in career and family attitudes.

In sum, this cohort enables us to examine the effects of both generational and life-cycle transitions, as well as differences associated with variations in life-course patterns and with the timing of life-course events. We begin our analysis by focusing on achievement orientation.

ACHIEVEMENT ORIENTATION

Analysis of this cohort further supports our primary hypothesis of stability in level of achievement orientation across the life cycle. In fact, the proportion of women with high achievement orientation varies by only 5.3 percentage points across all life-cycle groups (Table 5.2), suggesting that level

Table. 5.2. Ages 35–44: Achievement Orientation, Career Orientation, Career Values, Family Values, and Full-time Employment, by Life-Cycle Group

Life-Cycle Group	High Achievement Orientation (percent)	Career-Oriented (percent)	High Career Values (percent)	High Family Values (percent)	Employed Full-Time (percent)
Mar, presc	63.6	96.7	67.7	75.8	21.9
Mar, elem	61.4	86.7	61.4	68.9	36.1
Mar, youth	65.3	79.7	50.7	58.7	44.4
Sing, chil	65.5	95.7	90.7	44.2	77.0
Childless	66.7	97.1	85.7	14.7	80.0
	$\chi^2(4) = .216$	$\chi^2(4) = 12.71^*$	$\chi^2(4) = 30.34^{**}$	$\chi^2(4) = 41.89^{**}$	$\chi^2(8) = 60.17^{**}$

Note: The χ^2 statistics test the significance of the association between life-cycle group and each variable.

* $p = .013$.
** $p < .0001$.
Source: Prepared by author.

of achievement orientation does not rise or fall with transitions in family life-cycle stage.

One finding related to achievement orientation does, however, seem to suggest a generational transition occurring among the women in this cohort. Among the married mothers of preschool children, there is a relatively strong, although statistically nonsignificant, positive correlation between age at first birth and achievement scale scores (r= .31, p>.05). This suggests a tendency for the more highly achievement-oriented women in this group to delay childbearing. Such a relationship between age at first birth and achievement orientation was not evident, however, in the other groups of mothers in this cohort.

Moreover, the married mothers of preschool children are, on the average, the youngest group in this cohort. We thus begin to see a generational difference between the younger and older mothers in this cohort. These findings suggest that among the older women in this cohort, high achievement orientation was less likely to lead to definite career plans and a postponent of marriage and childbearing. Instead, the older women perhaps more often gratified their achievement needs, either directly or vicariously, through the traditional wife and mother roles. Among the youngest women in this cohort, however, changes in the social climate and in the possibilities of careers for women meant a change in the expression of achievement orientation.

CAREER ORIENTATION

Our findings related to career orientation, especially among the married mothers, suggest the occurrence of a generational transition among the women in this cohort. In light of the constraints and incentives of their marital and parental statuses, it is not surprising that a high proportion of the single mothers and childless women are career-oriented (Table 5.2). But more important, among married mothers, the proportion of women who are career-oriented is negatively related to age of youngest child (Table 5.2). And because age of youngest child is positively related to the average age of the mother in these three groups, this means that the youngest mothers (the mothers of preschool children) are the most likely to be career-oriented, while the oldest mothers (the mothers of adolescents and youth) are the least likely to be career-oriented. Further analysis shows that among all the mothers in this cohort, married and single, current age is negatively related to both age at first marriage and age at first birth. This means that, compared with the older women in this cohort, the younger women were more likely to marry and to begin childbearing relatively late.

These findings seem to reflect a generational shift toward increasing career orientation among the younger women. Moreover, the analysis further suggests that this generational transition toward increasing career orientation was accompanied by a willingness, or need, to delay marriage and childbearing in order to actualize career plans. Certainly this interpretation is supported by other data showing not only increasing career orientation among recent cohorts of college women (Cross 1975), but also national trends toward delayed marriage and chlidbearing among young women (see Huston-Stein & Higgins-Trenk 1978).

ATTAINMENT VALUES

Despite the narrow age span of this cohort, variations in attainment values reflect the effects of both generational and life-cycle transitions, as well as differences in life-course patterns. We find, first, relatively high career values among single mothers and childless women, reflecting the particular life-course patterns of the women in these groups. For some, including many single mothers, the need to earn a living may result in a strong career focus; for others, the desire to have a career may be an important determinant of marital and childbearing decisions. Both choice and necessity affect the life course, and our cross-sectional data do not allow us to determine the developmental sequence of career involvement and family status among the women in our sample. In general, however, individual attitudes and values reflect, as well as affect, one's position in the social structure (Berger 1963).

Among the three groups of married mothers, the relationship between career values and life-cycle group follows a pattern similar to that of career orientation. In these three groups, the proportion of women with high career values is negatively related to age, represented by age of youngest child (Table 5.2). Thus, compared with the older women in this cohort, the younger women are more likely not only to plan careers, but also to place a high value on career attainment. This pattern, reflecting the greater career interest of younger women, suggests a generational effect, and contrasts sharply with the life-cycle effect evident in the 22-34 cohort.

In the 22-34 cohort, the married mothers of preschool children were less likely than the other four life-cycle groups to have high career values. In fact, compared with the married mothers of preschool children, the married mothers of elementary school children were far more likely to have high career values, despite a negligible difference in achievement orientation. On the average, the 22-34-year-old mothers of elementary school children married and bore children at a relatively young age. It is thus unlikely that they were trained and highly career-involved during the demanding preschool family stage. Instead, their interest in career attainment probably rose sharply with the transition to middle motherhood, when the decline in family responsibilities allowed more outside involvement. In other words, in the 22-34 cohort, differences in career values reflect transitions in family life-cycle stage.

The explanation for the relationships observed in the 35-44-year-old cohort is different, however. If career values were determined primarily by family stage, then these values would be highest among the mothers of school-age children. Instead, the strongest career values are among preschoolers' mothers, who are the youngest life-cycle group. Thus we have strong evidence of a generational change. Among the youngest women in this cohort, achievement orientation and career orientation perhaps influenced decisions about the timing of marriage and childbearing. Indeed, on the average, the mothers of preschool children in this cohort married and began childbearing relatively late. It is likely that these women completed college on time and developed their career interests before and during the early years of marriage. They have thus maintained high career values during early motherhood.

In contrast, the older mothers in this cohort represent a generation who, in their youth, were less likely to plan to gratify their achievement needs through a career. Thus, their marital and childbearing decisions were not based on any long-range career goals. The extent to which they currently value career attainment is a more recent development, a product of social change and increased opportunities.

As in the 22-34 cohort, there is a significant relationship between family values and life-cycle group (Table 5.2). Compared with married mothers, single mothers are less likely to have high family values, perhaps because of their need to focus on the role of economic provider. Among married mothers, we find a negative relationship between age of youngest child and the proportion of women with high family values (Table 5.2). Thus, married women in the preschool family stage are most likely to have high famliy values, while married mothers of adolescents and youth are least likely to have high family values. This finding is particularly notable, considering the positive relationship between age of youngest child and average age of the mother in these three groups. In Chapter 3 we saw that age cohort is positively related to family values, reflecting a generational transition in the sample as a whole. Yet, in the three groups of married mothers in this cohort, it is the youngest women (the mothers of preschool children) who are most likely to have high family values.

The association between age of youngest child and family values thus reflects a strong life-cycle effect. Compared with their counterparts in the 22-34 cohort, the 35-44-year-old mothers of preschool children married and began childbearing relatively late. Yet, in both the 22-34 and 35-44 cohorts, it is the married mothers of preschool children who are most likely to have high family values. This suggests that childbearing assumes paramount importance to women during the preschool family stage, regardless of the mother's age or the timing of childbearing in her life.

A comparison of the variations in career and family values highlights the contrasting effects of generational and life-cycle transitions. With increasing age of youngest child, the proportions of women with high career values and high family values decrease by approximately the same amount (Table 5.2). Although the degree of change is similar, however, the declines seem to reflect different effects. The declining proportion of women with high family values suggests a life-cycle effect related to the growing independence of children and declining functions of the maternal role. At the same time, the declining proportion of women with high career values represents a generational effect, reflecting the older women's lower career interest and lack of earlier career planning

Nevertheless, these changes must be viewed in larger perspective. Despite the declining proportions, half of the oldest mothers have high career values, and over half have high family values. In a sense, the mothers of older youth represent the older generation in terms of maintaining high family values, and the younger generation with respect to developing career interest. Among the youngest mothers, three-fourths have high family values, and, despite heavy family responsibilities, two-thirds have high career values. These women thus reflect the younger generation's determination to have both career and family.

This interpretation of differences, focusing on a generational change toward assigning high value to both career and family attainment, is supported by life-cycle group variations on the combined career and family values variable (Table 5.3). Nearly half the mothers of preschoolers have both high career and high family values. The mothers of elementary school children, too, are more likely to value both areas highly than to give high priority to only one. In contrast, only a fifth of the oldest married mothers assign high value to both areas. Family outranks career for nearly two-fifths, with career predominating for less than a third. Thus, despite fewer child-care responsibilities, the older mothers are interested primarily in family concerns, while younger mothers are interested in both family and career attainment.

As in the 22-34 cohort, both single mothers and childless women tend to emphasize career over family. This suggests that for both groups, the structural constraints and incentives related to their marital and parental status are conducive to career involvement. Nevertheless, nearly two-fifths of the single mothers attach high value to both career and family attainment (Table 5.3).

EMPLOYMENT STATUS

When women's labor force participation rates began to rise in the 1940s, the greatest increase was among women over 35.

Table 5.3. Ages 35–44: Combined Career and Family Values, by Life–Cycle Group (percentage distribution)

Life-Cycle Group	High Career High Family (percent)	High Career Low Family (percent)	Low Career High Family (percent)	Low Career Low Family (percent)	Total (percent)	N
Mar, presc	45.2	22.6	32.2	0.0	100.00	31
Mar, elem	37.7	23.9	31.1	7.3	100.00	151
Mar, youth	20.0	30.7	38.6	10.7	100.00	75
Sing, chil	39.2	52.9	5.9	2.0	100.00	51
Childless	5.9	79.4	8.8	5.9	100.00	34

$\chi^2(12) = 69.33.$
p <.0001.
Source: Prepared by author.

And among mothers, the greatest increase was among those with school-age children. This trend continued until the 1960s, when the rates of younger mothers of preschool children began to show the greatest increase (U.S. Department of Labor, Women's Bureau 1975). Thus, in the 1970s, the labor force participation rates of women aged 35-44 showed smaller gains than the rates of women in the 25-34 age group. In the period from 1970 to 1978, the labor force participation rate of women aged 25-34 increased from 45 percent to 62.2 percent, a sharp change of 17.2 percentage points, while the rate of women aged 35-44 increased from 51.1 percent to 61.6 percent, a smaller change of 10.5 percentage points (U.S. Department of Commerce, Bureau of the Census 1980: Table 6-2, p. 46). Thus, toward the end of the 1970s, slightly over three-fifths of the women in each age group were labor force participants.

But for women of all ages, labor force participation is related to family status; and in our 35-44 cohort, actual employment rates reveal the effects of marital and parental status. As in the younger cohort, we find that single mothers and childless women have predictably high rates of full-time employment (Table 5.2). And among married mothers, variations in employment reflect the effects of both life-cycle and generational transitions. The rate of full-time employment is positively related to age of youngest child (Table 5.2). Moreover, the primary change in nonemployment occurs in the shift from the preschool stage to the elementary school stage. In fact, compared with the other two groups of married mothers, the mothers of preschool children are about twice as likely not to be employed. Of the mothers of preschool children, 46.8 percent are not employed, compared with 22.1 percent of the mothers of elementary school children and 23.6 percent of the mothers of adolescents and youth. The increase in rates of full-time employment and the sharp decline in rates of nonemployment in the shift from early to middle motherhood suggests a life-cycle effect, reflecting the marked reduction in child-care responsibilities that accompanies this transition.

In contrast, the rates of part-time employment suggest a generational effect. The mothers of preschool children and the mothers of adolescents and youth are about equally likely to be employed part-time: 31.3 percent of the mothers of preschool children, 41.8 percent of the mothers of elementary school children, and 32.0 percent of the mothers of adolescents and youth are employed part-time. On the average, the mothers of preschoolers married late, and many probably began careers before childbearing. For them, part-time employment may be a means of remaining involved in their careers during early motherhood. In contrast, for the mothers of older youth, relatively lighter family responsibilities make full-time employment much more feasible. Thus, their high level of part-time employment may reflect a generally lower level of career preparation, commitment, and interest.

CAREER ORIENTATION, CAREER VALUES, AND EMPLOYMENT

Earlier we observed that among the three groups of married mothers, the proportion of women who are career-oriented and the proportion with high career values decrease as the average age of the mother (and age of youngest child) increases. These findings provide evidence of a generational transition, reflecting the greater career interest of younger women. At the same time, however, the rate of full-time employment increases with increasing age of the mother. This reflects a life-cycle transition related to the change in child-care responsibilities during middle motherhood.

As a result of these contrasting trends, the greatest discrepancy between rate of full-time employment and both career orientation and career values occurs among the mothers of preschool children. These large discrepancies between career attitudes and employment status for women in early motherhood occurred in the 22-34 cohort as well. Compared with their younger counterparts, the 35-44-year-old married mothers of preschool children are more likely to be career-oriented, to have high career values, and to be employed full-time. Nevertheless, the degree of discrepancy between career attitudes and employment status is roughly the same in the two cohorts. Among the mothers of preschool children in both cohorts, the proportion of career-oriented women, and the proportion with high career values, exceed the full-time employment rate by approximately 75 and 45 percentage points, respectively. This suggests that

regardless of the mother's age or the timing of early motherhood in the life course, the responsibilities of the preschool
family stage have a marked inhibiting effect on the actualization of married women's career plans through full-time
employment.

Nevertheless, the degree to which deferral of career
plans represents choice or constraint may vary according to
the age of the mother or the timing of early motherhood in
the life course. In general, we would expect a feeling of
constraint during the preschool family stage to manifest
itself in overall life satisfaction. Thus, in the next sections
we will examine the relative life satisfaction of the life-
cycle groups in this cohort, and then compare the relative
satisfaction of our 22-34 and 35-44-year-old married mothers
of preschool children.

LIFE SATISFACTION

Prior research leads us to expect both similarities and
differences in levels of life satisfaction among the women in
this cohort. As we noted earlier, Campbell's (1975; Campbell
et al. 1976) national study found that after a drop in
satisfaction during the preschool stage, married mothers
became more satisfied with their lives as their children grew
older. Life satisfaction also increased among never-married
women after the age of 30, and childless wives over 30 were
at least as satisfied with their lives as married mothers of
the same age. The most dissatisfied group of women were
the divorced and separated, most of whom had children.

Both prior literature (e.g., Bernard 1975) and the results
of our own analysis of the 22-34 cohort in our sample suggest,
further, that married women vary in their response to the
transition from early to middle motherhood. Some welcome
the relief from constant child care, while others dread the
decline of a central life role. For those who derive their
primary satisfactions, including gratification of achievement
needs, from the maternal role, the transition may be especially difficult. When her youngest child starts school, the
unemployed achievement-oriented woman must decide how to
fulfill her achievement needs. Some women obtain vicarious
satisfaction through helping and participating in their children's school careers. Others turn to "volunteerism as surro-
gate career" (Bernard 1975:123).

For numerous married women, however, the transition to middle motherhood is accompanied by a decision to enter or reenter the labor force, on a part-time or full-time basis, and some embark on full careers. Indeed, paid employment is an increasingly important means of gratifying achievement needs for many women (Dubnoff, Veroff & Kulka 1978: note 1, cited in Hoffman 1979). In a sample of Washington state mothers, Nye (1974) found higher satisfaction of employed than nonemployed women during the active child-rearing years. Thus, among the married women in this cohort, most of whom have school-age children, satisfaction should be positively related to employment, especially for those with high career values.

Our analysis shows, in fact, that life satisfaction is relatively high, and does not vary significantly, across the five life-cycle groups in this cohort. In fact, the differences in average life satisfaction scores are negligible, ranging from 4.05 among childless women to 4.17 among the married mothers of elementary school children.

The similarity in satisfaction scores may be due, in part, to the greater degree of homogeneity in family life-cycle stage within this cohort, compared with the younger cohort. Despite their difference in marital status, for example, the single mothers resemble the married mothers with respect to stage of motherhood: most have school-age children.

Moreover, because of their stage of motherhood, the single mothers may be able to expand their role as economic provider. In fact, compared with the single mothers in the 22-34 cohort, the 35-44-year-old single mothers are more likely to be employed full-time (77.0 percent vs. 55.9 percent), and are slightly more likely to be career-oriented (95.7 percent vs. 93.8 percent) and to have high career values (90.7 percent vs. 81.8 percent). This suggests that, overall, these single mothers' interests are congruent with the demands of their situation, and the majority currently have jobs to fulfill those demands. As we saw in Chapter 4, the results of a study by Tcheng-Laroche and Prince (1979) suggest that with adequate incomes, women are likely to make a satisfactory adjustment to single motherhood. Thus, it is not surprising that the 35-44-year-old single mothers are as satisfied as the single mothers in the younger cohort, as well as the married mothers in their own cohort. The average life satisfaction scores of the 22-34 and 35-44-year-old single mothers are, respectively, 4.06 and 4.09.

Among the married mothers in this cohort, the similar levels of life satisfaction may be related to the timing of childbearing and child rearing in the life course. We noted earlier that for women who delay childbearing, there may be some difficulties in the adjustment to parenthood (Daniels & Weingarten 1982). Nevertheless, during the preschool family stage, the benefits related to delayed childbearing seem to outweigh the costs, especially for career-oriented women (Daniels & Weingarten 1982; Gluck et al. 1980; Rossi 1980). But studies (Daniels & Weingarten 1982; Rossi 1980) suggest, further, that later in the family life cycle, the younger the mother, the fewer the difficulties she is likely to have in coping with the children's adolescence.

In our 35-44 cohort, the married mothers of preschool children were relatively late, and the married mothers of adolescents and youth were relatively early, in marrying and beginning childbearing. Thus, both groups may be experiencing their respective stages of child rearing at the "ideal" time in the life course. If so, this would help to explain their similar, relatively high satisfaction levels.

When we compare the relative life satisfaction of the married mothers of preschool children in the 22-34 and 35-44 cohorts, we find further support for our hypothesis that the 35-44-year-old group is experiencing early motherhood at the more or less "ideal" time in the life course for this particular family stage. The average life satisfaction score of the 35-44-year-old married mothers of preschool children is 4.15, compared with an average score of 3.89 for their counterparts in the 22-34 cohort. In the next section, we will return to this difference in life satisfaction scores as we consider the implications of differences in the timing of the preschool family stage in women's lives.

Thus far we have seen that several factors may help to explain the similarity in satisfaction of the different life-cycle groups in this cohort. Nevertheless, significant differences in satisfaction may emerge when the effects of marital status and employment status are examined separately, especially when career and family values are included in the analysis.

Considering the effects of marital status, first, we find no significant differences in the life satisfaction of married and single women. Considering only those with high family values, however, the higher satisfaction of married than single women approaches statistical significance (F=2.916, p= .089). The similarity in satisfaction of married and single women may reflect several life-cycle changes. Never-married women become more satisfied with their lives as they get older, perhaps partially as a result of increasing rewards and gratifications from career involvement. Among married women, the happy honeymoon stage of marriage ends abruptly when children enter the scene (Campbell 1975). Furthermore, the period of active child rearing is, to some extent, a period of disengagement from the marital relationship per se. Much of the husband-wife interaction may center on their common concerns with the children (Cavan 1974), and satisfactions from family relationships decrease for the mother when the children enter school (Weiss & Samelson 1958). Compared with married mothers, childless wives over 30 have different, but relatively equivalent, sources of gratification (Campbell 1975). In short, during this age period, earlier differences between married and single women in potential sources of satisfaction even out. Since marriage is not as satisfying, single women are missing less.

The relationship between employment status and life satisfaction during this period is generally as predicted. The association is not significant among single women, but is significant and positive among married women (F= 5.398, p= .005). Furthermore, when career values are controlled, the relationship is significant among married women with high, but not low, career values (Table 5.4). Moreover, satisfaction for this group increases with full-time, but not part-time employment. This differs slightly from Nye's (1974) finding that the positive relationship between employment and satisfaction favored especially those employed part-time. Most high-level positions, however, require full-time commitment. Since many of the women in our sample are highly trained, their satisfaction may be enhanced only by jobs that utilize their full potential.

Table 5.4. Ages 35–44: One–Way ANOVA of Life Satisfaction by Employment Status, by Career Values: Married Respondents Only

Employment Status	Mean Life Satisfaction Score	N	F-Statistic	Probability	η^2*
		High Career Values			
Not employed	4.04	27	4.29	.015	.0516
Employed part-time	4.02	58			
Employed full-time	4.43	76			
		Low Career Values			
Not employed	3.97	39	.627	.536	.0122
Employed part-time	4.08	40			
Employed full-time	4.27	26			

*η^2 is a measure of association showing the proportion of variance in life satisfaction scores explained by employment status.
Source: Prepared by author.

108

FAMILY, CAREER, AND THE LIFE COURSE:
AN INTERCOHORT COMPARISON OF
THE PRESCHOOL FAMILY STAGE

In women's lives, the timing of marriage and motherhood is related to a number of other life-course events, including educational attainment and career involvement (see Huston-Stein & Higgins-Trenk 1978). Research suggests, further, that the timing of childbearing, particularly, is in turn related to degree of satisfaction with the various stages and experiences of motherhood (Daniels & Weingarten 1982; Rossi 1980). Indeed, the factors that affect the timing of childbearing, including degree of career involvement, also affect adjustment to motherhood (see, e.g., Fabe & Wikler 1979; Plunkett 1980). This suggests that during the preschool family stage, a woman's overall satisfaction will be related to a complex of factors involving career and family attitudes and employment status, as well as the timing of childbearing.

By comparing the married mothers of preschool children in our 22-34 and 35-44 cohorts, we may discover some of the implications of variations in the timing of marriage and motherhood in the life course. At the time of the present study, the married mothers of preschool children in the 35-44 cohort were, on the average, about six years older than their counterparts in the younger cohort (36.6 vs. 30.87 years old). Moreover, the older mothers had married, on the average, about 1.5 years later than their younger counterparts (23.38 vs. 21.77 years old), and were almost a year older at first birth (26.58 vs. 25.83 years old). While these average differences are not large, they may be critical, especially if the slight delays in marriage and childbearing allowed time for completion of college or graduate school, or for gaining a firm hold in a career field. At the same time, however, these averages should be seen in proper perspective: compared with women in the general population, the married mothers of preschool children in both cohorts were relatively late in marrying and beginning childbearing.

In career and family attitudes, employment status, and life satisfaction, there are small, but potentially important, differences between the 22-34 and 35-44-year-old married mothers of preschool children. Compared with their younger counterparts, the older mothers are somewhat more likely to be career-oriented (96.7 percent vs. 90.1 percent), to have high career values (67.7 percent vs. 59.2 percent), and to have the combination of high career and low family values (22.6 percent vs. 17.5 percent). This suggests that the older mothers are slightly more interested in career attainment. And, in accordance with their greater career interest, the older mothers are more likely to be employed full-time (21.9 percent vs. 13.8 percent), and less likely to be nonemployed (46.8 percent vs. 51.1 percent) or employed part-time (31.3 percent vs. 35.1 percent). Nevertheless, the older mothers are more likely to have high family values (75.8 percent vs. 71.7 percent) and to have the combination of both high career and high family values (45.2 percent vs. 40.5 percent), thus suggesting strong family orientation in addition to strong career interest.

There are at least two plausible explanations for the observed differences between the older and younger mothers of preschool children. First, the greater career interest of the older mothers may be related to an approaching life-cycle transition. Compared with the younger mothers, the older mothers are more likely to be in the latter stages of early motherhood, approaching the transition to middle motherhood. Anticipating this transition, they may be developing or resuming career interests and planning for the years of middle motherhood. At the same time, however, the older mothers' greater tendency to have high family values may be explained by their older age, reflecting the positive association between age and family values in the sample as a whole.

A second explanation for the observed differences in career and family values and life satisfaction focuses on the differences between the two groups of mothers in the timing of marriage and first birth. As we noted earlier, the older mothers married and began childbearing at a slightly older age than the younger mothers. Thus, it is likely that their career interest and involvement developed early, prior to the preschool family stage. Having gained a foothold in a career, they may have maintained this interest and, to some extent, involvement, throughout early motherhood. In this interpretation, then, the higher career interest and full-time employment rate of the older mothers represents a maintenance of career interest throughout the preschool family stage, rather than the resumption or development of career interest in the transition to middle motherhood.

The older mothers' greater tendency to have high family values, and their higher mean satisfaction scores, are consistent with this interpretation focusing on their slight postponement of motherhood. Indeed, although adjustment to parenthood may be somewhat difficult, career-oriented women who delay childbearing often find that early motherhood is deeply, and sometimes surprisingly, satisfying (Daniels & Weingarten 1982).

Moreover, while priority may be given to the maternal role, employment can be an important contributor to life satisfaction during the preschool family stage. In a recent study, Schwartz examined the career and family attitudes of ten part-time and ten full-time employed mothers of children 18-20 months of age. Of these women, 19 had delayed childbearing, and "15 out of 19 reported that the timing had been good" (1980:90). From these case studies, Schwartz (1980:91) concluded that

> ... it appears that for women with small children the maternal role and its responsibilities do take real precedence over the work role. A part-time job to earn some money, have contact with other adults and to maintain a sense of professional identity is perceived as ideal.

Similarly, in a comparison of 20 employed and 5 nonemployed mothers of preschool children, Plunkett (1980:96) found that "working outside the house gives a woman a sense of autonomy and competence which is different from what she experiences at home" and that "A second gratification ... gained from working was social contact with other adults."

In the present study, the older mothers of preschool children were more likely to be employed full-time, and slightly less likely to be employed part-time, than their younger counterparts. These older, largely career-oriented mothers of preschool children may prefer full-time employment, or part-time employment may be unavailable to them. At any rate, it is likely that the employment role is an important factor contributing to the greater satisfaction of the older mothers.

SUMMARY

The 35-44-year-old cohort includes single mothers, childless women, and married mothers of children from preschool to college age. Despite these variations in marital and parental status, there is little variance in achievement orientation, suggesting stability in achievement orientation across the life cycle.

There are, however, some important variations in this cohort that suggest a generational difference between the older and younger women. Among the youngest women in this cohort, there is a slight indication that high achievement orientation is related to postponement of childbearing. Furthermore, compared with the older mothers, the younger mothers are more likely to be career-oriented and to attach high value to both career and family attainment.

Employment status is closely related to marital and parental status, with the highest rate of full-time employment among single and childless women, and the highest rate of nonemployment among married mothers of preschoolers. Nevertheless, the mothers of preschool children and the mothers of adolescents and youth have a similar level of part-time employment, suggesting a higher degree of career commitment among the younger mothers.

Life satisfaction does not vary significantly among life-cycle groups in this cohort. This may be due partially to the counter-balancing of potential sources of satisfaction associated with different family statuses, and it may also be related to variations in the timing of childbearing and child rearing in the life course. Nevertheless, among married women with high career values, satisfaction is significantly related to full-time employment.

Comparison of the 22-34 and 35-44-year-old married mothers of preschool children supports other research suggesting that among career-oriented women, delayed childbearing may be associated with higher satisfaction during early motherhood.

6.

AGES 45-64:
THE LATE FAMILY STAGE

The attitudes and values of the women in this cohort, aged 45-64, reflect their life-cycle stages, their generation, and the interaction of these factors. Because they span an age range of 20 years, different conditions prevailed at the time of their birth and their entrance into adulthood. The oldest women were born before World War I and reached adulthood during the depression of the 1930s, while the youngest were born during the depression and reached adulthood during the early 1950s, the period of the "feminine mystique" (Friedan 1963). Despite these differences, however, the women in this cohort of our sample were influenced early by societal norms that dictated adherence to the traditional roles of wife and mother. For most, marriage and career were available only on "either-or" rather than "both-and" terms. If a young woman was employed, she generally withdrew from the labor force when she married, and often never returned (Chafe 1976). These societal values and expectations significantly shaped the childhood and early adulthood of the women of this period. Thus, even when new options became available, some women, particularly the oldest ones in this cohort, may not have sought employment or pursued a career because of their long-held beliefs about women's roles or a feeling "that it was too late ... to change" (Bardwick 1980: 53; see also Bernard 1981).

But life-cycle stage, as well as generation, affects the attitudes and values of women of this age cohort. A number of important issues confront women during the life-cycle stages covered by the years from 45 to 64. This is the period of children's departure, of the care and loss of elderly parents, and of impending retirement (Bardwick 1980; Gluck et al. 1980). These factors may be further complicated by divorce or the death of a spouse.

Surely one of the key events of this period, and one receiving a great deal of research attention, is the launching of children from the home. Technically, late motherhood begins when the youngest child leaves home. In reality, however, the transition from middle to late motherhood is accomplished gradually, as children enter the adult world through the period of extended adolescence known as "youth." Bernard (1975:113) summarizes the problems created by the extension of emotional and financial ties between parents and youth during this transitional period:

> The youth of sons and daughters straddles middle and late motherhood. The sons and daughters may be part of the new youth culture, supported still by subsidies from parents, but insisting on a life style quite at variance with parental, especially maternal, preferences.

Continuing emotional involvement, coupled with loss of control over children's behavior, creates special problems for women who obtained vicarious satisfaction from their children's accomplishments. Bart (1970) discovered that depression was often associated with maternal role loss among women who were "over-involved" with their children and achieved vicariously through them. More generally, the depression associated with the loss of the maternal role in late motherhood has been discussed as the "empty nest syndrome."

Bernard (1975) argues, however, that the "empty nest syndrome" is primarily characteristic of the generation of mothers born around the turn of the century. These women were socialized for a motherhood role that changed during their lifetime. Lengthening life expectancy, coupled with new household equipment, left this group of women with many hours to fill after the last child left home. Subsequent generations of mothers have been more apt to anticipate and prepare for the years of late motherhood. Increasingly, women are defining themselves less in terms of motherhood and becoming more involved in the community, continuing education, and the labor force. Thus, for many women, the onset of late motherhood signals a welcome liberation: "The 'hurrah' response to the empty nest is increasingly winning over the depressed one" (Bernard 1975:144).

A number of studies, including national survey data, support Bernard's assertion. Some studies suggest that among married women, satisfaction increases when the children leave home (Campbell 1975; Glenn 1975; Lowenthal 1975; Radloff 1975). Indeed, as we noted in Chapter 5, "prime time," from a woman's perspective, may begin with the empty nest (Bernard 1981).

Certainly, for many women, the freedom of the empty nest period affords greater opportunities for leisure, social activities, and attention to the marital relationship (Gluck et al. 1980). And for some women, this is the time to seek employment or to resume or begin a career (Bardwick 1980).

Moreover, in conjunction with some of the external events of this period, an important developmental change occurs that can interact with, and vitally affect, women's family and career activity. A number of studies indicate that around midlife, women become more assertive and autonomous, while men become more nurturant and affiliative (see Rossi 1980). This means, for one thing, that women may particularly enjoy career pursuits and employment at this stage. But the changes in both sexes can have important ramifications for the stability of a couple's marriage. Initially, conflict may arise as the needs and desires of both members change. Yet, if they are handled adequately, these changes may set the stage for a couple to work out a new complementarity in roles, leading to deeper satisfaction with the marriage.

How a woman chooses to invest her time when the children leave home is largely related to her age, in two ways. First, as we noted earlier, the older a woman was when new employment and career options become available, the less likely she is to pursue them (see Bardwick 1980:53). Further, a woman's behavioral response to the empty nest depends on her chronological age when her children actually leave. A woman who is in her forties when the children leave would be more likely than a woman in her fifties to respond with career involvement (Gluck et al. 1980:314).

While married women may generally respond positively to the freedom of late motherhood, this life-cycle transition may be much more difficult for the single mothers of this age (see Bardwick 1980:51). The occurrence of divorce and widowhood may be especially difficult for women of this cohort, because their generation was not prepared for economic independence (Barnett & Baruch 1980). It is these women who often experience the multiple problems of the "displaced homemakers" (see Bernard 1981:172-73).

For never-married and childless women, too, this stage in the life cycle has special concerns. The single career woman may confront both the death of her parents, to whom she may feel especially close (see Gluck et al. 1980), and the end of her career mobility (Bardwick 1980:50). And, once beyond childbearing years, women who chose to remain childless may have second thoughts. Currently, "it is . . . still not clear what the emotional sequelae are of voluntary childlessness in the later phases of the life span" (Rossi 1980:29).

Thus, whatever their marital and parental status, women aged 45-64 confront important life-cycle issues. Morever, as a result of social change, the experience of late motherhood itself is in a state of transition. Women currently in the launching phase and empty nest stage are likely, then, to reflect both old and new values and attitudes concerning the expression of achievement orientation during this period.

In the present study, the mothers in the 45-64-year-old cohort span the transition from middle to late motherhood. They may be differentiated by stage of motherhood (middle or late) and by marital status (married or single). In addition, this cohort includes a small group of married, never-married, and widowed childless women. Table 6.1 shows the number and percentage of women in each of the five life-cycle groups, and includes a detailed description of their marital and parental status. Of those in middle motherhood (groups 1 and 3), most are clearly in the launching phase, with their youngest child an adolescent. Only a fifth of the married mothers and a fourth of the single mothers in middle mother-

Table 6.1. Ages 45–64: Marital Status and Age of Youngest Child, by Life-Cycle Group

Group	Marital Status	N	Percent	Age of Youngest Child	N	Percent	Group N	Percent of Total Cohort[a]
(1)	Married mothers of children and youth (Mar, young)						128	34.32
	Married	128	100.00	1–5	1	0.78		
				6–12	26	20.31		
				13–18	101	78.91		
					128	100.00		
Total								
(2)	Married mothers of adult children (Mar, adult)						154	41.28
	Married	154	100.00	19–22	82	53.25		
				≥ 23	72	46.75		
					154	100.00		
Total								
(3)	Single mothers of children and youth (Sing, young)						28	7.51
	Separated/divorced	25	89.29	6–12	7	25.00		
	Widowed	3	10.71	13–18	21	75.00		
		28	100.00		28	100.00		
Total								
(4)	Single mothers of adult children (Sing, adult)						45	12.06
	Separated/divorced	33	73.33	19–22	26	57.78		
	Widowed	12	26.67	≥ 23	19	42.22		
		45	100.00		45	100.00		
Total								
(5)	Childless women (Childless)						18	4.83
	Married	6	33.33					
	Never married	9	50.00					
	Widowed	3	16.67					
		18	100.00					
Total								
Grand total							373	100.00

[a]Percentages were rounded to total 100 percent.
Note: The abbreviations in parentheses will be used in subsequent tables in this chapter.
Source: Prepared by author.

hood have a preadolescent child. Over half of those with adult children (groups 2 and 4) have at least one college age youth, and are thus in the earliest stage of late motherhood.

Information about the average age of the women in these five life-cycle groups will be useful in interpreting the results of our subsequent analysis. In average age, the married mothers of adult children ($\bar{X}$=54.18 years), the single mothers of adult children ($\bar{X}$=53.13 years), and the childless women ($\bar{X}$=54.78 years) are roughly similar. And these three groups are, on the average, approximately six to seven years older than the married ($\bar{X}$=48.90 years) and single ($\bar{X}$=47.71 years) mothers of young children and adolescents. Thus, we may speak of younger and older mothers, respectively, when referring to mothers in middle and late motherhood. Within this cohort, both age and marital status differences will be useful in considering generational and life-cycle effects on achievement-related attitudes and behavior.

ACHIEVEMENT ORIENTATION

In a nationally representative sample, Baruch (1967) found lower achievement motivation among women over 55. In her study of Radcliffe alumnae, however, the oldest women were 25 years out of college, and thus about 47 years old. Among the Radcliffe women, level of achievement motivation was similar for those 15 and 25 years out of college. In the present study, the oldest life-cycle groups are, on the average, slightly less than 55 years old. Thus, prior research leads us to expect stability, rather than decline, in achievement orientation from middle to late adulthood.

Table 6.2 indicates that level of achievement orientation does not vary significantly among life-cycle groups. Nevertheless, the range in proportion of women with high achievement orientation is 24.1 percentage points, from a high of 65.3 percent of the older married mothers, to a low of 41.2 percent of the childless women. Controlling for marital status, older mothers are slightly more likely than younger mothers to be highly achievement-oriented. This suggests a slight rise in achievement orientation from middle to late motherhood. Nevertheless, within each stage of motherhood, achievement orientation is higher among married than single mothers. Furthermore, childless women, two-thirds of whom are single, are lowest in achievement orientation.

This pattern of variance in achievement orientation among life–cycle groups can perhaps best be understood in terms of the women's achievement goals and the components of achievement orientation that we are measuring. Most of the women in this cohort were socialized in a culture that defined successful marriage and child rearing as women's most important achievements. Although many developed career interests later, their early and primary allegiance may be to the family. Two of the primary components of achievement orientation, measured in our scale, are a sense of personal efficacy and self–esteem about achievement. It is not surprising, then, that the married mothers of adult children, who have launched their children into the world and maintained an intact marriage, would score highest on this measure of achievement orientation. Women whose marriages were unsuccessful, or who currrently feel powerless in confrontations with independent adolescents, may have little sense of control and accomplishment. Those who never achieved the goals of marriage or motherhood may feel the least efficacious.

In this interpretation, we are assuming reciprocal effects of achievement orientation and position in the social structure. High achievement orientation leads to striving to reach achievement goals. At the same time, success in reaching these goals reinforces the sense of personal efficacy and the self-esteem that are primary components of achievement orientation.

Among women with traditional feminine goals, the effect of successful achievement on sense of personal efficacy may be greater than vice versa. Unfortunately, women have relatively little control in the areas and modes of achievement defined as appropriate for them. In the area of family, for example, accepted norms and traditions have frequently limited the expression of women's initiative in determining whether and when they marry. Furthermore, success in child rearing is generally defined in terms of the child's, not the mother's, behavior. Women's socialization to be vicarious achievers makes them dependent for a sense of accomplishment on the behavior of husbands and children, over whom they have only limited control. Thus, among older women with traditional goals, achievement orientation may be as much an effect as a cause of life events.

CAREER ORIENTATION

Within this cohort, the proportion of career-oriented women varies little across life-cycle groups (Table 6.2), and compared with the younger cohorts, these proportions are relatively low (compare Tables 4.2, 5.2, and 6.2). For example, in the youngest cohort, the lowest rate of career orientation was 90.1 percent, occurring among the married mothers of preschool children (Table 4.2), while the highest rate of career orientation in the 45-64 cohort is only 85.7 percent, occurring among the single mothers of children and youth (Table 6.2). Thus, the intercohort differences in career orientation are most prominent, showing a generational transition toward career planning among younger women.

Nevertheless, there are small intracohort differences in career orientation associated with both age and marital status. Within each marital status category (married vs. single), younger mothers are more likely than older mothers to be career-oriented, perhaps suggesting a slight generational transition even within this cohort. Moreover, when stage of motherhood (launching vs. postparental or "empty nest"), and thus age, is held constant, single mothers are more likely than married mothers to be career-oriented. The similar, relatively high proportion of career-oriented women among the younger single mothers and childless women probably reflects the factors associated with their marital and parental status. For many single women, necessity is a strong incentive, and for childless women, the family constraints are relatively few, for career development.

ATTAINMENT VALUES

In general, career and family values vary little among the groups in this cohort, suggesting generational homogeneity. Compared with the younger women, the women in this cohort are less likely to have high career values, and more likely to have high family values.

Career values do not vary significantly across life-cycle groups, and reflect the relatively low career interest of older women (Table 6.2). For example, in this cohort, the proportion of single mothers with high career values is from 20 to 37 percentage points lower than the proportion of single mothers with high career values in the 22-34 and 35-44 cohorts (compare Tables 4.2, 5.2, and 6.2).

Nevertheless, among the mothers in this cohort, the slight variance in career values resembles the pattern we observed for career orientation; that is, there are differences associated with both age and marital status. Thus, within categories of marital status (married vs. single), the younger mothers are slightly more likely than the older mothers to have high career values (Table 6.2). Again, as with career orientation, this difference between the younger and older mothers may reflect a slight intracohort generational transition toward greater career interest among younger women.

Alternatively, these differences in career values between younger and older women may suggest that declining career interest accompanied the family life-cycle transition from the launching stage to the "empty nest" or postparental stage of late motherhood, at least within this particular cohort of women. As Rossi (1980) noted, many of today's middle-aged women never intended to work outside the home, but closely spaced births and large families, coupled with the increasing importance of a college education, propelled some of them into the labor force to meet the educational and other economic needs of their families. For such women, the importance of a career would be likely to decline when all the children are launched from the home.

But career values are related to marital status as well as age. When we compare groups of mothers of the same age, but different marital status, we find that single mothers are slightly more likely than married mothers to have high career values (Table 6.2). This difference no doubt reflects the greater economic constraints and the inducements for career involvement among single women. Nevertheless, despite these slight variations related to age and marital status, career values generally reflect relatively low career interest among the women in this cohort.

In contrast, family values reflect a relatively high degree of family involvement and interest among the four groups of mothers in this cohort. About two-thirds of the women in each group of mothers have high family values (Table 6.2). Indeed, the mothers in this cohort are only slightly less likely to have high family values than the married mothers of preschool children in the two younger cohorts (compare Tables 4.2, 5.2, and 6.2). Thus, even in the

Table 6.2. Ages 45–64: Achievement Orientation, Career Orientation, Career Values, Family Values, and Full–time Employment, by Life–Cycle Group

Life–Cycle Group	High Achievement Orientation (percent)	Career–Oriented (percent)	High Career Values (percent)	High Family Values (percent)	Employed Full–Time (percent)
Mar, young	58.9	78.9	53.6	70.0	48.0
Mar, adult	65.3	69.6	45.6	67.3	43.3
Sing, young	48.1	85.7	61.5	66.7	63.0
Sing, adult	60.5	79.4	53.7	66.7	63.6
Childless	41.2	84.6	53.3	12.5	66.6
	$\chi^2 (4) = 5.94$	$\chi^2 (4) = 4.95$	$\chi^2 (4) = 3.37$	$\chi^2 (4) = 21.26^*$	$\chi^2 (8) = 11.86$

Note: The χ^2 statistics test the significance of the association between life–cycle group and each variable.

* p = .0003.

Source: Prepared by author.

122

late family stages, the family is a central area of achievement concern among the older, less career-oriented women.

The interest in family rather than career is also clear from the distribution of combined career and family values. Although the mothers in this cohort are generally in later family stages, they are as likely as the mothers in the younger cohorts to value attainment in family more than career (compare Tables 4.3, 5.3, and 6.3). Indeed, only a fifth to a fourth of each group of mothers in the 45-64 cohort emphasize career over family, despite the reduction in child-care responsibilities during this life stage (Table 6.3).

This pattern of high family and low career values, and the contrasts between the 45-64-year-old mothers and the mothers in the younger cohorts, emphasize the generational transition evident in our sample. The career and family attitudes of the older women reflect the world into which they were born and in which they experienced their early socialization (see Bernard 1981:127), a socialization that generally emphasized family roles and did not encourage preparation for careers and economic independence (see Barnett & Baruch 1980). Decisions about career and family, emanating from early socialization and societal opportunity structures, established life patterns not easily changed (Huston-Stein & Higgins-Trenk 1978). As noted previously, after the establishment of their families, some women in the older cohorts were pushed into the labor force because of economic need (Rossi 1980). Some even developed an interest in, and pursued training for, careers. Nevertheless, the earliest and primary identification of many of these women is with family roles. Thus, they continue to emphasize family interests over career concerns even during the launching and empty nest phases of late motherhood.

The lack of career emphasis and preparation in women's traditional socialization is further reflected in the combined career and family values of the childless women in this cohort. In accordance wtih their marital and parental status, over half of the childless women value career over family. Yet, a third of the childless women rank low on both dimensions (Table 6.3). For this small group of five women (one-third of the 15 childless women), interest in a career apparently did not develop despite the relative lack of certain family constraints.

Table 6.3. Ages 45–64: Combined Career and Family Values, by Life–Cycle Group (percentage distribution)

Life-Cycle Group	High Career High Family (percent)	High Career Low Family (percent)	Low Career High Family (percent)	Low Career Low Family (percent)	Total Percent	N
Mar, young	31.7	21.7	38.3	8.3	100.00	120
Mar, adult	21.5	23.6	45.1	9.8	100.00	144
Sing, young	36.0	24.0	32.0	8.0	100.00	25
Sing, adult	30.0	25.0	35.0	10.0	100.00	40
Childless	0.0	53.3	13.4	33.3	100.00	15

χ^2 (12) = 26.04.
p = .01.
Source: Prepared by author.

EMPLOYMENT STATUS

The ages of 45-64 are potentially a woman's most active years of continuous labor force participation. At that time, women are generally freed from family responsibilities for more physical and emotional investment in a career. Increases in both longevity and career interest, as well as current trends in labor force participation, suggest that women will increasingly be employed throughout this period.

Among women who are currently aged 45-64, however, labor force participation is affected by old norms and patterns that limited their previous work experience and career training. Thus, despite the reduction in child-care responsibilities that accompanies the transition to late motherhood, older women are less likely to be employed than younger women. In 1978, for example, almost three-fifths (57.1 percent) of U.S. women aged 45-54 were in the labor force, a rate just slightly lower than that of women aged 25-34 (62.2 percent) and 35-44 (61.6 percent). Yet, in that same year, only 41.4 percent of the 55-64-year-old women were in the labor force (U.S. Department of Commerce, Bureau of the Census 1980: Table 6-2, p. 46).

The generally lower participation rates of older women are also reflected in a comparison between the mothers of adult and school-age children. In 1977, among married women (husband present) with no children under 18 years old, 44.9 percent were in the labor force, compared with 55.6 percent of the married women with children aged 6-17 (U.S. Department of Commerce, Bureau of the Census 1978: no. 657, p. 405).

But despite these differences in the overall labor force participation of older and younger women, marital status has a similar effect on the participation rates of both groups. In 1977, 44.6 percent of the married women (spouse present), 67.6 percent of the single woman, and 58.5 percent of the separated, divorced, and widowed women in the 45-64 age group were in the labor force (U.S. Department of Commerce, Bureau of the Census 1978: no. 656, p. 404).

Several factors help to account for the lower participation rates of older women. For one thing, the physiological effects of aging affect the relationship between age and employment status (Sweet 1973). And, as noted previously, women in the 45-64 age bracket are less likely to have previous labor force experience, and lack of prior experience decreases the likelihood of current employment (Sweet 1973). Then, too, although reduction in child-care responsibilities may encourage labor force participation, the reduced need for supplementing the family income, once the children are out of college, may discourage it, particularly among women whose generation was not trained for careers.

Within this cohort of our sample, it is primarily marital status, rather than age, that affects the variation in the labor force participation of life-cycle groups. The groups with older average ages (single and married mothers of adult children and childless women) do not all show higher full-time employment rates than the groups with younger average ages (single and married mothers of children and youth). Instead, we find that approximately two-thirds of the single and childless women, compared with less than half of the married women, are employed full-time (Table 6.2). Perhaps the age effect is not evident here because the average age of each life-cycle group is less than 55, and nationally, women's employment rates drop in the 55-64 age category.

Comparisons across cohorts, however, do suggest a generational effect on labor force participation. In some comparable groups of younger women, many of whom have greater family responsibilities, the rates of full-time employment equal or exceed those of the groups in this cohort. For example, in the youngest cohort, 47.2 percent of the married mothers of elementary school children, compared with 43.3 percent of the married mothers of adult children in this cohort, are employed full-time (compare Tables 4.2 and 6.2). Similarly, approximately four-fifths of the single mothers and childless women in the middle cohort, compared with only about two-thirds of these groups in this cohort, are employed full-time (compare Tables 5.2 and 6.2). Thus, our sample reflects the generational shift toward increasing labor force participation during the earlier and more demanding stages of the family life cycle.

CAREER ORIENTATION, CAREER VALUES, AND EMPLOYMENT

Compared with the two younger cohorts, there is less intra-cohort variation in career orientation, career values, and full-time employment among the 45-64-year-old women. Thus, there is also less variation in the degree of discrepancy between career attitudes and employment status among the life-cycle groups in this cohort. This reflects both generational and life-cycle stage homogeneity among the women in this cohort.

The actual size of the discrepancy between the proportion of women who are career-oriented and the proportion with high career values ranges from 24.0 to 31.3 percentage points across life-cycle groups (Table 6.2). Since the mothers in this cohort are beyond the early child-rearing stages, when family concerns compete with career involvement, such large discrepancies are particularly notable. While many of the women in this cohort regard themselves as having a career, they do not assign great importance to it. This relative lack of investment in a career, despite reduction in family responsibilities, perhaps reflects this cohort's membership in a generation for whom career preparation was not primary. The discrepancies between career attitudes and actual employment status, examined below, support this interpretation.

For all groups in this cohort, the proportion of women who are career-oriented is greater than the proportion employed full-time (Table 6.2). Nevertheless, the degree of discrepancy between career orientation and employment is smaller among single and childless women, whose incentives for employment are likely to be high. And in these three groups, the rate of full-time employment actually exceeds the proportion of women with high career values.

This suggests that among the single and childless women, particularly, the need for employment outweighs interest in and investment in a career. In fact, many older women who were not planning to pursue careers have found that employment is necessitated by their marital status, life-cycle stage, or life-course pattern. The need for employment, combined with lack of interest in and preparation for a career, has the potential for creating personal strain and distress. Indeed, because of lack of training for economic independence, older divorced and widowed women are particularly vulnerable to economic distress (see Barnett & Baruch 1980), which can, in turn, negatively affect overall life satisfaction. By comparing the satisfaction of married and single women, we will explore this possibility further in the next section.

LIFE SATISFACTION

Although loss of the maternal role may contribute to middle-age depression among some women (Bart 1970), Bernard (1975) has suggested that the "empty nest syndrome" is primarily characteristic of the generation of women born early in the twentieth century. Indeed, a recent study revealed

> ... that the empty nest transition has, at most, a rather slight and transitory effect on the psychological well-being and essentially no effect on the physical well-being of mothers (Harkins 1978:555).

Other investigations have shown that among married women, satisfaction increases, rather than decreases, when the children leave home (Campbell 1975; Glenn 1975; Lowenthal 1975; Radloff 1975). For example, Campbell's comparison of life-cycle groups in a national sample revealed that

> ... parents of older children were among the happiest groups of the study, and this was true for both sexes. Couples settled back in the "empty nest" reported feelings of companionship and mutual understanding even higher than they felt as newlyweds (1975:39).

This suggests that with maternal role loss, marriage becomes more important to life satisfaction. The same study (Campbell 1975) found that both widows and divorced and separated women were extremely negative about the emotional quality of their lives. Furthermore, although widows and older (>30 years) never-married women were more generally satisfied than the divorced and separated, none of them were as satisfied as older married women.

Marriage is likely to be especially important to satisfaction for this older cohort of women. Most of these women were socialized to expect marriage, and they had fewer objective career and job opportunities as viable alternatives to marriage. For the single mothers in this cohort, especially, dissatisfaction may arise from lack of preparation and support for dealing with the economic exigencies of single, independent living (Allan 1975; Barnett & Baruch

1980; Barrett 1979). Moreover, a recent investigation (Douvan 1978, cited in Kaufman & Richardson 1982:121) comparing the results of national surveys found that never-married women surveyed in 1957 had more positive attitudes toward marriage than never-married women surveyed in 1976. This suggests that it is the older never-married women who are more likely to feel that they have missed an important and satisfying life role.

We would also expect employment to become more essential to satisfaction as the function of motherhood declines. In his study of Washington mothers, however, Nye (1974) found that older mothers were happier if they were not employed. He attributed this somewhat puzzling finding to the lower educational level of these women, resulting in a greater likelihood that those who were employed held menial, low-paying jobs.

Nevertheless, among college-educated women, there is evidence that employment is related to greater satisfaction during late motherhood. For example, Powell (1977) examined a sample of 40 "empty nest" married women in their late fifties, all of whom had graduated from an eastern women's college 35 years prior to the study. In this investigation, which used a scale to measure psychiatric impairment, "Women employed full-time were found to have significantly lower symptom scores than women not employed outside the home, with women employed part-time occupying an intermediate position" (Powell 1977:35). Thus, in our relatively highly educated sample, we would expect a positive relationship between employment and satisfaction during the later family life-cycle stages.

In sum, as in the younger cohorts, prior research suggests that marital status, stage of motherhood, and employment status are the pertinent variables to explore for their effects on the life satisfaction of women in this older cohort.

In the first stage of our analysis, we compared the mean life satisfaction scores of the women in the five life-cycle groups. The results of this analysis suggest that marital status, rather than age of youngest child, is the more important determinant of life satisfaction for women in this age cohort. The mean life satisfaction score of the single mothers of adult children ($\bar{X}=3.86$) is not markedly higher than the mean satisfaction score of the single mothers of adolescents and younger children ($\bar{X}$=3.68). Similarly, the score of married mothers of adult children ($\bar{X}$=4.30) is virtually the same as the score of the married mothers of preadult children ($\bar{X}$=4.25). Thus, in contrast with both the "empty nest syndrome" and "sigh of relief" notions of late motherhood, these data do not suggest a marked change in satisfaction level when the children are gone.

Nevertheless, the slight differences in the satisfaction levels of the mothers of adult and preadult children are consistent with prior data regarding the timing of parenthood in the life course. As we noted earlier, delaying childbearing can be particularly advantageous for the young woman attempting to establish a professional career. But later, when the children reach adolescence, prior data suggest that the older the mother, the more likely she is to have difficulty during this period (Rossi 1980). This may be particularly true for single mothers, who often lack both emotional and financial support for the difficult tasks of rearing, supporting, and launching adolescents and youth. In fact, compared with the younger single mothers, the single mothers in this cohort are less likely to have been prepared for economic independence, while the financial burdens of the adolescent and launching periods are particularly great. Thus, the single mothers of preadult children in this cohort are likely to experience some of the stress and dissatisfaction that prior research has found among divorced and separated women (e.g., Campbell 1975).

But as the scores themselves indicate, marital status has a greater effect than stage of motherhood on satisfaction. Compared with the single mothers, the married mothers have markedly higher mean life satisfaction scores. And the mean satisfaction score of childless women ($\bar{X}$=3.88), two-thirds of whom are single (see Table 6.1), resembles that of the single mothers.

Controlling for level of attainment values helps to clarify further the effects of marriage on satisfaction. First, we find that among those with high family values, single women are significantly less satisfied than married woman (Table 6.4). As Bernard (1981:171-172) suggests, from a woman's point of view, the "world of the formerly married" (Hunt 1966) is likely to be the world of the "displaced homemaker." Bernard (1981:172) enumerates some of the difficulties often confronting a woman when she divorces:

Table 6.4. Ages 45–64: One-Way ANOVA of Life Satisfaction by Marital Status, by Family Values and Career Values

Marital Status	Mean Life Satisfaction Score	N	F-Statistic	Probability	η^2*
		High Family Values			
Single	3.74	47	12.43	.0005	.0515
Married	4.34	184			
		Low Family Values			
Single	3.97	33	.272	.603	.0023
Married	4.09	88			
		High Career Values			
Single	4.14	44	.769	.382	.0043
Married	4.29	136			
		Low Career Values			
Single	3.33	33	18.07	< .0001	.0956
Married	4.24	140	18.07	.0001	.0956

*η^2 is a measure of association showing the proportion of variance in life satisfaction scores explained by marital status.

Source: Catherine A. Faver, "Life Satisfaction and the Life Cycle: The Effects of Values and Roles on Women's Well–Being," Sociology and Social Research 66 (July 1982): 435–451, Table 7. Copyright 1982 by the University of Southern California Press. Reprinted by permission.

With divorce she encounters the legal framework of marriage and finds to her dismay that her rights are few if any and that the contributions she has made to her husband's career or to the household are not considered to give her a vested right in his estate. Alimony is usually not granted. . . . Child-support payments, even when allotted, are rarely enforced.

Widows, according to Bernard (1981:175) confront similar difficulties:

Even at best, the status of widowhood has its own legal disabilities for women. The law specifies their rights of inheritance. In some cases they suffer serious injustice.

In short, divorce and widowhood are difficult not only emotionally but also financially. This is especially true among 45-64-year-old women with high family values. Having invested their lives in family concerns, they are not prepared for economic independence. Their skills and experience are not valued in the job market, and they confront "ageism" and other legal and economic barriers to achievement (see, e.g., Allan 1975; Bart 1975; Sontag 1975). Not surprisingly, then, the women with high family values in this cohort are particularly dependent on marriage for life satisfaction.

Yet, our analysis also suggests that career interest and involvement may reduce the effect of marriage on the satisfaction level of women in this cohort. Marriage significantly increases the satisfaction of women with low, but not high, career values (Table 6.4). Moreover, satisfaction is positively and significantly related to paid employment among married women with high career values (Table 6.5). Thus, our data suggest that among career-oriented, middle-aged women, marriage is neither necessary nor sufficient for a fully satisfying life.

These findings suggest that the worker role may provide an alternative source of satisfaction, as well as financial support, as women confront maternal, and often marital, role loss in their middle age. Admittedly, gratifications from work and from marriage may not be "equivalent." Indeed,

Table 6.5. Ages 45–64: One-Way ANOVA of Life Satisfaction by Employment Status, by Career Values: Married Respondents Only

Employment Status	Mean Life Satisfaction Score	N	F-Statistic	Probability	η^2*
		High Career Values			
Not employed	3.41	22	12.39	< .0001	.1581
Employed part-time	4.25	28			
Employed full-time	4.54	85			
		Low Career Values			
Not employed	4.06	48	.935	.395	.0141
Employed part-time	4.32	47			
Employed full-time	4.33	39			

*η^2 is a measure of association showing the proportion of variance in life satisfaction scores explained by employment status.

Source: Catherine A. Faver, "Life Satisfaction and the Life-Cycle: The Effects of Values and Roles on Women's Well-Being," Sociology and Social Research 66 (July 1982): 435–451, Table 8. Copyright 1982 by the University of Southern California Press. Reprinted by permission.

survey data suggest that family is somewhat more important than occupation to both men and women (Campbell et al. 1976; Erskine 1973). Nevertheless, these findings offer further support for the "dual role hypothesis" (see Gove & Tudor 1973; Radloff 1975) that employment may offer alternative gratifications when satisfactions from family roles decline.

Earlier we saw that women with high family values were especially dependent on marriage for satisfaction. Thus, to the extent that their satisfaction is tied to the marital relationship, the well-being of these family-centered homemakers may be quite tenuous. Their vulnerability to sudden loss of spouse suggests the need for other sources of satisfaction, and a variety of structural supports, to ease the transition to single status. While paid employment may not be desired or needed by every woman at mid-life, appropriate structural supports should be instituted in order to make employment a viable alternative for each woman who chooses it.

Finally, our findings are suggestive for life satisfaction among childless women. Earlier we noted the increase in voluntary childlessness among recent cohorts of young women (Blake 1979; Huston-Stein & Higgins-Trenk 1978). In his national survey, Campbell (1975) found that childless wives over age 30 were at least as satisfied with their lives as married mothers of the same age. As we noted earlier, however, "the emotional sequelae . . . of voluntary childlessness in the later phases of the life span" are still unknown (Rossi 1980:29).

In our sample, we have no way of distinguishing between the voluntarily and involuntarily childless, although the older women in the sample are less likely to have chosen childlessness. Moreover, the effect of childlessness on satisfaction may be confounded by the effect of marital status. Nevertheless, it may be useful to compare the relative satisfaction of the childless women in the three age cohorts.

In the 22-34 cohort, the mean life satisfaction scores revealed that single childless women were one of the two least satisfied groups ($\bar{X}=3.92$), while married childless women were the most satisfied group ($\bar{X}=4.39$) in their cohort. While the single childless women may be anxious about fulfilling the cultural expectation or their personal desire to marry, the married childless women are perhaps enjoying the honeymoon stage of marriage. At any rate, many women in both groups may be planning eventually to become mothers.

In the 35-44 cohort, two-fifths of the 40 childless women are married, almost two-fifths are never-married, and slightly over a fifth are separated or divorced (see Table 5.1). As we noted in Chapter 5, these women do not differ significantly from the other life-cycle groups in their cohort in mean satisfaction score ($\bar{X}$=4.05).(1) And, while they are somewhat less satisfied than the 22-34-year-old married childless women, they are, nevertheless, slightly more satisfied than the 22-34-year-old single childless women. This may suggest that an adequate adjustment has been made to both marital and parental status.

Yet, as we have seen, in the 45-64-year-old cohort the small group (N=18) of childless women resembles single mothers in their relatively low mean life satisfaction score ($\bar{X}$=3.88).(2) Since two-thirds of the 45-64-year-old childless women are single, however, it is difficult to know whether their low satisfaction, compared with married mothers, is related primarily to marital status, parental status, or other factors. But it is nevertheless notable that the 45-64-year-old childless women are somewhat less satisfied than the childless women in the two younger cohorts. This finding underscores the vulnerability of women who are currently middle-aged in American society. Of course, having children is not a guarantee against loneliness in one's middle and later years. Nevertheless, prior research (Lopata 1979) shows that adult children are an important point of contact and source of social support for many widows. This suggests that childless women are more susceptible to isolation, particularly upon loss of spouse. Thus, for childless women particularly, employment may be important as a buffer against loneliness and isolation during late middle age.

SUMMARY

Although this cohort includes a small group of childless women, it consists primarily of single and married mothers of adolescent and adult children. During these late stages of motherhood, marital rather than parental status is the structural factor most strongly affecting achievement attitudes and behavior. Compared with the middle cohort, there is greater generational homogeneity within this cohort.

Achievement orientation does not vary significantly among life-cycle groups, despite a slight rise from middle to late motherhood. In this cohort, variations in level of achievement orientation may be a reflection of the extent to which women in the different groups have been successful in fulfilling traditional roles.

Among the life-cycle groups in this cohort, career orientation and career values follow a similar pattern and reflect the effects of both age (generation) and marital and parental status (life-cycle stage and life-course pattern). Women who are single, childless, or younger are more likely to be career-oriented and to have high career values. Moreover, despite their late stages of motherhood, about two-thirds of each group of mothers have high family values, reflecting their generation. Indeed, the mothers in this cohort are as likely as the mothers of younger children to value family over career attainment.

Marital status has the greatest effect on employment status. Compared with married mothers, single mothers and childless women are more likely to be employed full-time. Since family responsibilities have declined during this period, age and marital status exert the primary effects on the channeling of achievement orientation and on the expression of career orientation and career values in paid employment.

There is no evidence for a strong change in life satisfaction when the children are launched from the home. Instead, life satisfaction is associated with marital and employment status. Among those with high family or low career values, married women are more satisfied than single women. Furthermore, the association between satisfaction and paid employment is strongest among married women with high career values.

NOTES

1. The mean life satisfaction score of the childless women in the 35-44 cohort is based on an N of 39.
2. The mean life satisfaction score of the childless women in the 45-64 cohort is based on an N of 17.

7.

SUMMARY, CONCLUSIONS, AND IMPLICATIONS

SUMMARY

The patterns of women's labor force participation and career activity have been strongly shaped by their roles as wives and mothers. Prior research maintained that women's achievement motivation, too, follows a temporal cycle associated with age and family status (Baruch 1967). Our research tests an alternative hypothesis: that women's achievement orientation is actually stable during adulthood, but that the areas in which it is expressed depend on age (as an indicator of generation), life-cycle stage, and life-course pattern.

The data for the study were derived from a mailed questionnaire study conducted in 1977 by the University of Michigan Center for Continuing Education of Women. The subjects were a cross-sectional, nonprobability sample of 1,120 women, aged 22-64, who contacted the Center between 1964 and 1973. Compared with a national probability sample, the CEW sample included a larger proportion of white, highly educated, relatively affluent women.

Stages in the individual life course and the family life cycle are conceptualized as positions in the social structure and defined in terms of age and marital and parental status.

Approximately one-third of the sample is included in each of three cohorts defined by the age categories 22-34, 35-44, and 45-64. Within each cohort, life-cycle groups are differentiated by marital status and age of youngest child.

The results of the present study suggest, first, that the level of women's achievement orientation is stable during adulthood. We observed that level of achievement orientation does not vary significantly among women in three age cohorts and a variety of life-cycle stages. These findings thus contradict the prior research reporting associations between changes in the level of women's achievement orientation and both family life-cycle stages and employment patterns (Baruch 1967). Asserting stability in women's achievement orientation, the present study suggests that the relationship between women's employment patterns and family life-cycle stages may not be attributed to life-cycle changes in level of achievement orientation.

Yet, while the level of achievement orientation remains stable, the expression of women's achievement orientation varies with age and marital and parental status, reflecting both generational and life-cycle transitions. Thus, we emphasize the importance of historical location and structural position in channeling the expression of women's achievement orientation.

Career orientation is negatively related to age cohort. Younger women are more likely to have, or plan, careers, and the relationship between achievement orientation and career orientation is stronger among younger than older women. This suggests a generational transition toward the expression of women's achievement orientation through career activity.

Furthermore, career values (the values attached to career attainment) are more likely to be high among women who are young, single, childless, or beyond the preschool family stage. Family values, in contrast, are more likely to be high among women who are older, married, or the mothers of preschool children. Yet, young married mothers are especially likely to value both career and family attainment.

The present study indicates that women's high valuation of both career and family attainment persists into adulthood, even during the demanding stage of early motherhood. This supports and expands earlier research indicating an increase in young women's aspirations for both career and family (Cross 1975).

Nationwide patterns of women's labor force participation are evident in our sample. Married mothers of school-age children, as well as single and childless women, are more likely to be employed than married mothers of preschool children. Furthermore, intercohort comparisons of employment rates suggest a generational shift toward increasing labor force participation during the early family stages. Nevertheless, both age and life-cycle stage affect the extent to which career orientation and career values are expressed through labor force participation.

The greatest discrepancy between level of career values and rate of full-time employment occurs among married mothers of preschool children, whose child-care responsiblities are likely to be greatest. This suggests that, during early motherhood, structural constraints inhibit the actualization of young women's career values through full-time employment.

Positions in the social structure vary in the opportunities they provide for achieving through career and family. Thus, for women of all ages and life-cycle stages, we expected life satisfaction to depend on the fit between individual attainment values (the importance assigned to achievement in a given area) and structural position.

The data supported this hypothesis. In accordance with prior research, we found that satisfaction is higher among married than single women, and among employed than non-employed women. More important, women's career and family values emerged as important mediators of the relationship between their work and family statuses and life satisfaction. Thus, in the sample as a whole, satisfaction is positively related to employment among those with high, but not low, career values. Similarly, marital status is significantly related to satisfaction only among those with high family values or low career values. In general, these findings suggest that satisfaction is relatively lower among those whose value orientation is incompatible with the structural constraints or requirements of their marital, parental, or employment status. Women tend to fare best when their roles allow for the expression of their individual values.

CONCLUSIONS AND IMPLICATIONS

Women's career orientation, career and family values, and employment status are strongly related to their position in the social structure--that is, their age and marital and parental status. Thus, when comparing women in different structural positions, we see reflected the effects of two types of transitions in women's attitudes and behavior: the transition from one generation to another, and the transitions that individual women experience as they move through the life course.

Level of achievement orientation, however, appears to be relatively stable, both across generations and across the life course. This is a highly significant finding. As Kaufman and Richardson (1982) suggest, the level of women's actual achievements has been underestimated through a failure to consider their great contributions in the private and domestic sphere. Similarly, much prior literature has failed to consider that women may express their achievement orientation in the private, as well as the public, sphere.

In contrast, the present study distinguishes between the level of women's achievement orientation and its expression in the areas of career and family. In this way, we demonstrate that a transition is occurring primarily in the expression of women's achievement orientation. We find that women are increasingly interested in channeling their achievement orientation into career attainment.

In certain ways, our study reflects important trends and transitions that are occurring in American society at large. For example, our data reflect the generational transition toward increasing career interest among women, and increasing labor force participation at earlier stages of the life cycle. Fox and Hesse-Biber (1984:200-01) summarize these trends as they are occurring nationwide:

> Work outside the home is becoming the norm for American women as it is for men; and perhaps most notably, labor force participation is becoming the norm for mothers as well .... In addition, responses to national surveys indicate that women view work as central to their lives and that they would choose employment even if they could manage comfortably without earned

income (Kamerman and Kahn, 1981:25). All this points toward a trend of permanent or lifetime labor force commitment and attachment for women--similar to that of men.

But despite these trends in employment attitudes and behavior, our data also suggest that structural constraints strongly inhibit the actualization of women's career values through full-time employment, especially during early motherhood. Thus, paradoxically, our study findings reflect not only social change but also a degree of stability in societal norms and patterns. And in this way, too, our data reflect the larger picture of what is occurring, and failing to occur, in American society:

> . . . despite these changes in labor force patterns, social institutions continue to be geared toward the traditional family model . . . . employment institutions continue to operate as though households had just one full-time worker and the supportive services of a full-time homemaker. Sex-role values continue to emphasize the dominance of husband's employment needs and opportunities. And housework and child care are still allocated disproportionately to women, whether they are employed or not. In this way, we have lags in values and social institutions, which have not kept pace with changes in labor force behavior (Fox and Hesse-Biber 1984:179).

In the present study, we noted that disjunctions between women's value orientations and social roles result in lower life satisfaction. On a larger scale, these disjunctions between individual values and roles may be related to, and even attributable to, the failure of certain social values and institutions to keep pace with social change, as Fox and Hesse-Biber (1984) described above. Thus, both our data and the national trends suggest the need for structural changes to enhance women's well-being.

It should also be noted that, compared with our CEW sample, less affluent women in the general population have even fewer options and resources with which to resist the power of structural forces. At the same time, they are just as varied in individual talents, goals, values, and preferences.

To the extent that there is a lack of fit between attainment values and opportunities to express them, women of all classes may be expected to feel keenly the restrictiveness of the social structure.

Nevertheless, because life satisfaction is a function of both individual values and structural opportunities for their expression, social interventions can significantly alter women's opportunities to achieve a satisfying fit between their values and roles. Essentially, the interventions suggested in the following sections are all aimed at achieving economic independence and occupational equity for women in American society, because many of the constraints on women's choices and opportunities derive from their "less than equal" status in these areas. But achieving economic and occupational equity requires changes in all social institutions. According to Fox and Hesse-Biber (1984:219):

> Only by altering basic institutional arrangements will we lift the constraints upon both the aspirations and ... the opportunities of American women at work.

Thus, interventions are aimed at the structures of family and household, education, and the polity as well as employment.

These changes in the structural arrangements of society would benefit women of all ages and life-cycle stages. Moreover, because of our interrelationships and interdependency as a society and as individuals, these changes would benefit men and children as well. But these structural changes are especially critical for particular groups of women. For, as the present study suggested, certain life-cycle stages, structural positions, and life-course patterns render women vulnerable to incongruities between value orientations and role opportunities. Our findings on three such groups are briefly reviewed below, and form the basis for a discussion of structural changes necessary to alleviate the disjunction between values and roles.

In this discussion, we will rely heavily on Fox and Hesse-Biber's (1984: ch. 9) elaboration of the various interventions and strategies necessary to achieve equity for women in the labor force. The reader is thus directed to Fox and Hesse-Biber for a more detailed discussion of specific structural changes and policy alternatives. The goal in the following discussion is to briefly indicate some of the problems that should be addressed and to suggest the aims toward which structural changes and policy formulation and revisions should be directed.

Single Women in Young Adulthood

In Chapter 4 we found that young single women had relatively low life satisfaction scores, particularly if they had low career or high family values. These findings directly reflect the structural constraints and realities confronting women in young adulthood. First, it is not surprising that young women in American society would approach adulthood with low career and high family values, since as we noted earlier, an individual's aspirations in a given area, as well as his or her actual achievements, are limited by the objective opportunities for achievement that are available (Kanter 1977). Traditionally, American society has defined marriage and motherhood as the most appropriate and highly valued achievement goals for women. And because of limited career opportunities, a sex-segregated labor market, and sex-inequality in pay structures, women's best economic prospects have been through marriage. As Tangri (1975:242, cited in Kaufman and Richardson 1982:141) suggests,

> ... marriage is the only kind of status for which women may legitimately strive, ... Marriage, or a particular kind of marriage, may be thought of as an achievement goal for women in much the same sense as a man's vocational choice serves as an achievement goal for him, ...for most women the determining influence of life style, opportunities, and limitations derives from the men they marry.

Moreover, despite the sharp increase in women's labor force participation and increasing career orientation among young women, Kaufman and Richardson maintain that there has been little change in the importance of marriage for women (1982:138):

> Marriage is as much an economic necessity at the end of the twentieth century as it was at the

> beginning. In the last half of this century, a woman alone (especially given the returns on her marketplace endeavors) still risks not only the stigma of social deviance but, clearly, economic deprivation as well. . . . Under these conditions the decision to marry reflects economic necessity as much as an enduring commitment to the private gender roles associated with marriage.

We could easily anticipate that young women whose marriage hopes are unfulfilled and whose career aspirations are constrained by structural realities would be relatively dissatisfied.

The connection between women's economic well-being and their marital status may be broken only by economic and occupational equity for the sexes. Already there is considerable evidence indicating that highly educated and high-income women are less likely to be married (see, e.g., Havens 1973; Hacker 1979, cited in Kaufman and Richardson 1982: 140). Moreover, as we have seen, career aspirations rise to the level of available opportunity (Kanter 1977).

Thus, the available evidence suggests that greater employment opportunities for women would raise their career aspirations, reduce the economic pressure to marry, and, in this way, enhance the overall well-being and life satisfaction of young single women. This supposition is supported by data from the present study indicating that in the sample as a whole, single women with high career values were not significantly less satisfied than married women (see Chapter 3). It should also be noted that increased career opportunities would facilitate women's maximum contribution to society, as well as benefit the women themselves.

As we suggested earlier, achieving occupational equity for women depends on changing not only the structure of employment itself, but also family and household, educational, and political structures (Fox & Hesse-Biber 1984: ch. 9). For young single women, the most pertinent changes are those aimed at altering educational, employment, and political structures.

First, changes are needed in the educational structures that constrain, limit, and channel women's aspirations and opportunities prior to reaching young adulthood (Fox &

Hesse-Biber 1984: chs. 3, 9). Indeed, sex–differential experiences and processes in education "are ... reflected in women's occupational 'choices' and 'preferences' and ultimately in their concentration in ... traditionally female-typed occupations ... " (Fox & Hesse-Biber 1984:204). Thus:

> ... strategies must redress the practices that directly segregate and track males and females into different curriculum groups and activities. Strategies must redress also the more indirect and implicit messages of texts, teachers, and staff that socialize the sexes into different occupational outcomes (Fox & Hesse-Biber 1984:204).

Second, the achievement of occupational equity for women necessitates interventions into the economic and employment structures themselves. Fox and Hesse-Biber (1984:220) summarize the most important of these intervention strategies:

> 1. The development of salary policies and standards of equal pay for comparable effort, skill, and responsibility 2. Open posting and standardized criteria for the recruitment, hiring, and promotion of personnel 3. Affirmative action to advance women and break the preferential hiring of men 4. Open lines of mobility from clerical and other jobs that currently have short promotion ladders and low ceilings on pay and prestige 5. Introduction of flexible work schedules and part-time options 6. The organization of women into unions and introduction of women and their causes into union leadership.

Finally, however, changes in the other basic structures of society depend upon changes in political institutions. Interventions into political structures must be directed toward identifying and redressing the practices that restrict women, and actively monitoring and enforcing the laws and statutes that ensure economic and occupational equity (Fox & Hesse-Biber 1984: ch. 9).

Married Mothers of Preschool Children

In Chapter 4 we found that married mothers of preschool children not only were the least satisfied group in the youngest cohort, but also were especially dissatisfied if they had high career or low family values (see Table 4.4). Moreover, considered together with our findings regarding the strong career orientation and relatively high career values in this group, the low satisfaction of these young mothers suggests that the responsibilities of early motherhood exert a strong constraint on women's labor force participation.

As in the case of young single women, the dissatisfaction of young mothers reflects current conditions and structural realities of American society. On the individual level, the dissatisfaction of many young mothers of preschoolers results from the disjunction between their high career values and traditional family role responsibilities. But on a larger scale, the failure of societal values and structures to keep pace with the increase in women's labor force participation creates, as Fox and Hesse-Biber (1984:201) note:

> ... a fundamental problem--of tension between work and home for people who want or expect children, and for the whole society, which if it is to survive, needs these children (Kamerman and Kahn, 1981; Land, 1980).

In our sample, this tension is reflected in the low labor force participation rates of young mothers of preschoolers, despite their high career values, and in their relatively low satisfaction level.

As we noted in Chapter 4, our findings suggest that structural changes aimed at facilitating women's career participation, while providing societal support for the care and rearing of children, could enhance the satisfaction of women during early motherhood. Indeed, such structural changes are essential and critically important, for as the above quotation suggests, the survival and well-being of the entire society are at stake.

Yet, although individual solutions to the problems created by the tensions between work and family are inadequate (Fox & Hesse-Biber 1984: ch. 8), on the societal level, the United States has not yet developed a national child-care policy (Fox & Hesse-Biber 1984:201-02).

In the previous section, we enumerated a number of structural changes needed to broaden and increase women's opportunities in the labor force, and thus enhance the satisfaction level of young single women. The suggested changes would, of course, reduce constraints, enhance career opportunities, and ensure equitable rewards for married women as well. But, in addition, the special problems and unique constraints experienced by mothers, particularly during the preschool family stage, necessitate a number of interventions directed specifically at the structure of family and household, and the interplay between family and work. Essentially, what is needed are "alternative ways for adults of both sexes to manage family and work roles without damage to themselves or the children" (Fox & Hesse-Biber 1984:219).

A national child-care policy must be developed to facilitate parenting and provide for the nurture and care of children. According to Fox and Hesse-Biber (1984: ch. 9), the two basic alternatives for child-care policy are benefits (cash or in-kind payments) and services. Examples of benefits include cash maternity benefits, child-care allowances, social insurance, and tax benefits. Among the benefits, one notable example is a six-month maternity leave that legitimizes shared parenting by allowing the parents to divide the leave between them (Safilios-Rothschild 1974:22, cited in Fox & Hesse-Biber 1984:201).

The second policy alternative, services for the out-of-home care of infants and children, includes the options of care in a household and care in a center. While research indicates that out-of-home care is not harmful to children or families, further evaluative research is needed on various types of care (Fox & Hesse-Biber 1984: ch. 9). And, in sum, there is a "pressing national need for the investigation and provision of childcare--either through the operation, subsidy, regulation, and/or licensing of these services" (Fox & Hesse-Biber 1984:219).

Whether child care takes the form of benefits, services, or both, such provisions would help to alleviate women's disproportionate share of household responsibility (Fox & Hesse-Biber 1984: ch. 9). In this way, a national child-care policy would reduce the stress of early motherhood and facilitate labor force participation and career pursuit for those who desire it.

Beyond the development of a national child-care policy, certain changes in the structure of employment would be particularly beneficial to mothers, especially during the early child-rearing years. As we noted in Chapter 4, some young mothers find that part-time employment enables them to strike an ideal balance between mothering and professional involvement during the early child-rearing years (see, e.g., Schwartz 1980). Thus, mothers of young children would benefit from changes that expand part-time opportunities and, in general, introduce greater flexibility in the structure of employment. In this regard, Fox and Hesse-Biber's (1984: 215) enumeration of innovations to improve the labor market status of part-time work is particularly pertinent to the plight of young mothers. These innovations include the establishment of flexible work schedules and part-time options in better-paying positions. In addition, part-time employment should offer the benefits of full-time work: pensions, insurance, seniority, vacations, and leaves of absence. Finally, some specific scheduling options are listed (Fox & Hesse-Biber 1984:215).

> (1) alternatives of work during part of the year, the month, the week, or the day; (2) flex-time, which provides for flexible starting and finishing times, but requires workers to be on the job during certain core hours; (3) job-sharing, which allows one position to be allocated between two persons; and (4) child care leaves for both men and women.

Single Women in Middle Adulthood

In Chapter 6 we found that among 45-64-year-old women with high family values or low career values, single women were significantly less satisfied with their lives than married women. Such a finding is not surprising in light of the cultural and structural realities of these women's lives. In American society, many women of their generation were reared to expect a life of homemaking and mothering (see Bernard 1975:140-41; Bernard 1981:127). Their values reflect this orientation. But such a gender role socialization, resulting in low career and high family values, did not prepare these women for economic independence (see Barnett & Baruch 1980; Kaufman & Richardson 1982:130). Thus, when the spouse is lost through death or divorce, many of these women become "displaced homemakers," vulnerable to economic as well as emotional distress.

But we also found that among 45-64-year-old women with low family values, and especially among those with high career values, single women were not significantly less satisfied than their married counterparts. Furthermore, among married women with high career values, life satisfaction was positively and significantly related to paid employment. Together, these findings suggest that career interest and involvement may make marriage less essential to life satisfaction, and may help to ease the transition to single status at midlife. The benefits of career involvement include not only financial support, but also opportunities to meet the needs for achievement and social support outside of the family context. Yet, women of this age bracket face a number of structural barriers to employment, particularly if they have little or no previous labor force experience. Thus, structural supports are needed to facilitate the labor force participation and career involvement of women at midlife.

Compared with older women, younger women are more likely to be career-oriented and to have continuous employment experience. The structural changes in education, employment, family, and the polity suggested above can facilitate occupational equity for future generations of women. Thus, in the long run, career development during early adulthood may reduce women's vulnerability to the economic and emotional stresses currently associated with marital role loss and single motherhood occurring at subsequent life stages.

But for middle-aged, family-centered women currently confronting divorce, widowhood, and single motherhood, some specific structural interventions are needed to ensure equity in society and to ease the transitions of middle life. In general, structural changes for this group should have two broad aims: first, they should facilitate the labor force participation of women at midlife; second, they should acknowledge the value of women's nonmarket labor, including especially their contributions to society through home and family (see Hauserman 1980; Kaufman & Richardson 1982). Some of the needed structural interventions merit further emphasis and elaboration.

First, structural changes are needed to facilitate the labor force participation of midlife women. Equal pay for work of comparable value, equity in recruitment and hiring, and the establishment of lines of mobility from low-paying jobs (see Fox & Hesse-Biber 1984:210-14) are critical for women in midlife, given the economic vulnerability and limited employment histories of many displaced homemakers.

The issue of equal pay for work of comparable value is especially important for midlife women (Kaufman & Richardson 1982:134). Compared with jobs in which men predominate, jobs in which women predominate have been undervalued and underpaid. Thus, in order to achieve salary equity for women, female-typed jobs must be reassessed on the basis of some neutral principle, and equal pay must be awarded for work of comparable effort, skill, and responsibility (Fox & Hesse-Biber 1984:211-12).

Kaufman and Richardson (1982:134) cite three specific reasons why the issue of comparable worth is especially critical to mature women. First, the establishment and enforcement of comparable worth standards can result in back pay and double indemnity, which, for women with long employment histories, can be sizable amounts. Second, since the existing job training programs for women frequently channel them into low-paying, low-mobility positions, the reassessment of the worth of these jobs is critical. Finally, given their socialization and early experiences, many mature women prefer, and feel more comfortable in, traditionally female-typed jobs and occupations (see Lenhoff 1980 and Lopata & Steinhart 1971, cited in Kaufman & Richardson 1982:134).

Because women are concentrated in low-paying positions, the establishment of lines of mobility from these jobs (see Fox & Hesse-Biber 1984:211, 214) is likewise a critical issue for midlife women. And with regard to standards and criteria for hiring and recruitment, there must be strict enforcement of laws against job discrimination on the basis of age as well as of sex (Allan 1975).

In addition to these changes in the structure of employment, further assistance and support are needed to facilitate the actual transition from home to employment (Hauserman 1980; Kaufman & Richardson 1982: ch. 5). Although some job training programs are available to women seeking to enter or reenter the labor force, these programs are limited in both number and scope. In general, they prepare women only for low-paying positions. Moreover, many mature women are overqualified for the positions for which training is provided (Kaufman & Richardson 1982: ch. 5).

A FINAL WORD

It is important to emphasize that the goal of structural changes and interventions is not to replace old structures with new, but equally rigid, family and work patterns. In fact, such a procedure is likely to exacerbate, rather than alleviate, distress. Instead, the goal of these suggestions is to broaden career and family opportunities for women of all ages and life-cycle stages. This means that the emphasis on recognizing the value of homemakers' nonmarket labor is important not only for women who are currently "displaced homemakers," but also for women (and men) of all ages and life-cycle stages, both now and in the future. Only when the value of homemaking and child rearing is recognized by society will women and men have the opportunity to devote substantial time and energy to family and home endeavors without severe economic penalty. The care and rearing of children, and the provision of a healthy family environment, are essential to all of society.

More generally, an emphasis on maximizing career and family opportunities for both men and women is critically important on both theoretical and substantive grounds. Recall, first, a basic finding of the present study: Among women of each age and life-cycle stage, life satisfaction is a function of the degree of congruence, or "fit," between individual values and roles. Similarly, the results of several studies suggest that "Power over the timing and sequencing of one's roles may be a key to mental well-being" (Kaufman & Richardson 1982:125). By maximizing choices and opportunities, we can enhance the probability that individuals will achieve a satisfying fit between their values and roles.

But there are also several substantive reasons for the importance of maximizing opportunities for participation in family, as well as career, roles. First, survey data suggest that family is a more important source of gratification than employment for both men and women (see Campbell et al. 1976; Erskine 1973; Hesselbart 1978, 1980). Moreover, recent evidence suggests that among both men and women, there is a decreasing willingness to sacrifice family interests and relationships for personal career and economic concerns (see Yankelovich 1981). Then, too, individuals investing their energies in career or family because of choice, rather than constraint, are more likely to enhance not only their own well-being, but also the happiness and satisfaction of their families and associates. And, at the same time, individuals with more alternatives are more likely to make choices that will maximize their contribution to society as a whole.

The present study of women in transition points, finally, to an entire society in transition. As with individuals, transitions in societies create both stress and opportunities for growth. In this particular period of change, the present study suggests that the creation of flexible and responsive societal institutions can facilitate a satisfying and beneficial outcome of transition for both individuals and society.

APPENDIX

CONSTRUCTION OF THE ACHIEVEMENT ORIENTATION, CAREER VALUES, FAMILY VALUES, AND LIFE SATISFACTION VARIABLES

I. Questionnaire Items

    A. Achievement Orientation Scale

        1. I am able to do things as well as most other people.(a)
        2. There's not much use for me to plan ahead because something always makes me change my plans.(b)
        3. When I do a job, I do it well.(a)
        4. I nearly always feel pretty sure of myself even when people disagree with me.

    B. Career Values Scale

        1. For me, it is (would be) more important to help my husband in his career than to have a career of my own.(b)
        2. Seriously pursuing a career involves costs in other areas of my life that I am not willing to accept.(b)
        3. I can't picture having a fully satisfying life without a career of my own.

    C.   Family Values Scale

        1.   The rewards and satisfactions of raising a family are more important to me than anything else.
        2.   I would not take a job that would interfere with the things I like to do with my family.
        3.   I can't imagine having a fully satisfying life without having children.

    D.   Life Satisfaction Measure

        1.   I think of my life today as interesting and satisfying.

(a) Source of item: Bachman & O'Malley (1977).
(b) Item was reverse-scored.

II.   Scoring Procedure

The responses to each item were scored according to the following five-point scale:

1 - Disagree
2 - Mostly disagree
3 - Neither agree nor disagree
4 - Mostly agree
5 - Agree

For the three scales, scores on individual items were averaged so that the possible scores for each scale ranged from 1 to 5, with high scores representing, respectively, high achievement orientation, high career values, and high family values. The possible scores on the life satisfaction measure also ranged from 1 to 5, with high scores representing high satisfaction.

III.   Dichotomous Variables

The four-item achievement orientation scale was divided at its mean to create the dichotomous achievement orientation variable. The dichotomous career values variable was constructed from the three-item career values scale. Mean scores in the agree/mostly agree range represented high career values, and mean scores in the neutral-to-disagree range represented low career values. The dichotomous family values variable was created by the same procedure as the dichotomous career values variable.

Note: The items on the achievement orientation, career values, and family values scales are reprinted from Faver (1981). Copyright 1981 by Sage Publications, Inc. Used by permission.

REFERENCES

Allan, Virginia R. 1975. "Economic and Legal Status of the Older Woman." In No Longer Young: The Older Woman in America, pp. 23-30. Ann Arbor/Detroit: University of Michigan/Wayne State University, Institute of Gerontology.

Almquist, Elizabeth M. Shirley S. Angrist, and Richard Mickelsen. 1980. "Women's Career Aspirations and Achievements: College and Seven Years After." Sociology of Work and Occupations 7 (August): 367-84.

Angrist, Shirley S., and Elizabeth M. Almquist. 1975. Careers and Contingencies: How College Women Juggle with Gender. New York: Dunellen.

Aronson, Elliot. 1980. The Social Animal. 3rd ed. San Francisco: W. H. Freeman.

Astin, Helen S. 1977. "Continuing Education and the Development of Adult Women." In Counseling Adults, pp. 135-49. Edited by Nancy K. Schlossberg and Alan D. Entine. Monterey, Calif.: Brooks/Cole.

Astin, Helen S., and Alan E. Bayer. 1975. "Sex Discrimination in Academe." In Women and Achievement: Social and Motivational Analyses, pp. 372-95. Edited by Martha T. S. Mednick, Sandra S. Tangri, and Lois W. Hoffman. Washington, D.C.: Hemisphere Publishing.

Atkinson, John W., ed. 1958. Motives in Fantasy, Action and Society. Princeton, N.J.: Van Nostrand.

Bachman, Jerald G., and Patrick M. O'Malley. 1977. "Self Esteem in Young Men: A Longitudinal Analysis of the

Impact of Educational and Occupational Attainment." Journal of Personality and Social Psychology 35 (June): 365-80.

Bakan, D. 1966. The Duality of Human Existence. Chicago: Rand McNally.

Baltes, Paul B., Steven W. Cornelius, and John R. Nesselroade. 1977. "Cohort Effects in Developmental Psychology: Theoretical and Methodological Perspectives." In Minnesota Symposium on Child Psychology. Vol. XI, pp. 1-63. Edited by W. A. Collins. Minneapolis: University of Minnesota Press.

Bardwick, Judith M. 1980. "The Seasons of a Woman's Life." in Women's Lives: New Theory, Research & Policy, pp. 35-57. Edited by Dorothy G. McGuigan. Ann Arbor: University of Michigan Center for Continuing Education of Women.

___. 1979. In Transition. New York: Holt, Rinehart and Winston.

Barnett, Rosalind and Grace Baruch. 1980. "Toward Economic Independence: Women's Involvement in Multiple Roles." In Women's Lives: New Theory, Research & Policy, pp. 69-83. Edited by Dorothy G. McGuigan. Ann Arbor: University of Michigan Center for Continuing Education of Women.

Barrett, Carol J. 1979. "Women in Widowhood." In Psychology of Women: Selected Readings, pp. 496-506. Edited by Juanita H. Williams. New York: W.W. Norton.

Bart, Pauline B. 1975. "Emotional and Social Status of the Older Woman." In No Longer Young: The Older Woman in America, pp. 3-21. Ann Arbor/Detroit: University of Michigan/Wayne State University, Institute of Gerontology.

___. 1970. "Mother Portnoy's Complaint." Trans-Action 8 (November-December): 69-74.

Baruch, Rhoda. 1967. "The Achievement Motive in Women: Implications for Career Development." Journal of Personality and Social Psychology 5 (March):1966 260-67.

Battle, Esther S. 1966. "Motivational Determinants of Academic Competence." Journal of Personality and Social Psychology 4 (December): 634-42.

___. 1965. "Motivational Determinants of Academic Task Persistence." Journal of Personality and Social Psychology 2 (August):209-18.

Berger, Bennet. 1960. "How Long is a Generation?" British Journal of Sociology 11 (March):10-23.

Berger, Peter L. 1963. Invitation to Sociology: A Humanistic Perspective. Garden City, N.Y.: Doubleday/Anchor Books.

Berkman, Paul L. 1969. "Spouseless Motherhood, Psychological Stress and Physical Morbidity." Journal of Health and Social Behavior 10 (December):323-34.

Bernard, Jessie. 1981. The Female World. New York: The Free Press.

___. 1975. Women, Wives, Mothers: Values and Options. Chicago: Aldine.

___. 1974. The Future of Motherhood. New York: Penguin Books.

___. 1971. Women and the Public Interest: An Essay on Policy and Protest. Chicago: Aldine.

Birnbaum, Judith A. 1975. "Life Patterns and Self-Esteem in Gifted Family Oriented and Career Committed Women." In Women and Achievement: Social and Motivational Analyses, pp. 396-419. Edited by Martha T.S. Mednick, Sandra S. Tangri, and Lois W. Hoffman. Washington, D.C.: Hemisphere Publishing.

Blake, Judith. 1979. "Is Zero Preferred? American Attitudes Toward Childlessness in the 1970s." Journal of Marriage and the Family 41 (May):245-57.

Bram, S. 1974. "To Have or Have Not: A Social Psycho-logical Study of Voluntarily Childless Couples, Parents-to-Be, and Parents." Ph.D. dissertation, University of Michigan.

Brim, Orville G. 1976. "Theories of the Male Mid-Life Crisis." Counseling Psychologist 6:3-16.

Briscoe, C. William, James B. Smith, Eli Robins, Sue Marten, and Fred Gaskin. 1973. "Divorce and Psychiatric Dis-ease." Archives of General Psychiatry 29 (July):119-25.

Campbell, Angus. 1981. The Sense of Well-Being in America: Recent Patterns and Trends. New York: McGraw-Hill.

____. 1980. "Changes in Psychological Well-being During the 1970s of Homemakers and Employed Wives." In Women's Lives: New Theory, Research & Policy, pp. 291-301. Edited by Dorothy G. McGuigan. Ann Arbor: University of Michigan Center for Continuing Education of Women.

____. 1975. "The American Way of Mating: Marriage Sí, Children Only Maybe." Psychology Today 8 (May):37-43.

Campbell, Angus, Philip E. Converse, and Willard L. Rodgers. 1976. The Quality of American Life: Perceptions, Evaluations, and Satisfactions. New York: Russell Sage Foundation.

Campbell, Jean W. 1973. "Women Drop Back In: Educa-tional Innovation in the Sixties." In Academic Women on the Move, pp. 93-124. Edited by Alice S. Rossi and Ann Calderwood. New York: Russell Sage Foundation.

Cavan, Ruth S. 1974. "Family Life-Cycle, United States." In Marriage and Family in the Modern World: Readings, pp. 91-104. Edited by Ruth S. Cavan. 4th ed. New York: Thomas Y. Crowell.

Chafe, William H. 1976. "Looking Backward in Order to Look Forward: Women, Work and Social Values in America." In Women and the American Economy: A Look to the 1980s, pp. 6-30. Edited by Juanita M. Kreps. Englewood Cliffs, N.J.: Prentice-Hall.

Chester, Robert. 1971. "Health and Marriage Breakdown: Experience of a Sample of Divorced Women." British Journal of Preventive and Social Medicine 25:231-35.

Condry, John, and Sharon Dyer. 1976. "Fear of Success: Attribution of Cause to the Victim." Journal of Social Issues 32 (Summer):63-83.

Coser, Rose L., and Gerald Rokoff. 1971. "Women in the Occupational World: Social Disruption and Conflict." Social Problems 18 (Spring):535-54.

Crandall, Vaughn J. 1963. "Achievement." In Child Psychology: Sixty-second Yearbook of the National Society for the Study of Education, pp. 416-459. Edited by Harold W. Stevenson. Chicago: University of Chicago Press.

Crandall, Vaughn J., Walter Katkovsky, and Anne Preston. 1962. "Motivational and Ability Determinants of Children's Intellectual Achievement Behaviors." Child Development 33:643-61.

Crandall, Vaughn J., Anne Preston, and Alice Rabson. 1960. "Maternal Reactions and the Development of Independence and Achievement Behavior in Young Children." Child Development 31 (June):243-51.

Crandall, Virginia C., and Esther S. Battle. 1970. "The Antecedents and Adult Correlates of Academic and Intellectual Achievement Effort." In Minnesota Symposia on Child Psychology. Vol. IV, pp. 36-93. Edited by John P. Hill. Minneapolis: University of Minnesota Press.

Cross, K. Patricia. 1975. "Women as New Students." In Women and Achievement: Social and Motivational Analyses, pp. 339-54. Edited by Martha T. S. Mednick, Sandra S. Tangri, and Lois W. Hoffman. Washington, D.C.: Hemisphere Publishing.

Daniels, Pamela, and Kathy Weingarten. 1982. Sooner or Later: The Timing of Parenthood in Adult Lives. New York: W. W. Norton.

Denmark, Florence L., Sandra Schwartz Tangri, and Susan McCandless. 1978. "Affiliation, Achievement, and Power: A New Look." In The Psychology of Women: Future Directions in Research, pp. 393-460. Edited by Julia A. Sherman and Florence L. Denmark. New York: Psychological Dimensions.

Disch, Estelle. 1977. "Troubled Single Women in Early Adulthood: Issues and Strategies." Paper presented to the Eastern Psychological Association, April.

Douvan, Elizabeth. 1978. "Family Roles in a Twenty Year Perspective." Paper presented to the Radcliffe Pre-centennial Conference, Cambridge, Mass., April.

Dubnoff, S. J., J. Veroff, and R. A. Kulka. 1978. "Adjustment to Work: 1957-1976." Paper presented at the meeting of the American Psychological Association, Toronto, August.

Elder, Glen H., Jr. 1975. "Age Differentiation and the Life Course." In Annual Review of Sociology, Vol. I, pp. 165-90. Edited by Alex Inkeles, James Coleman, and Neil Smelser. Palo Alto, Calif.: Annual Reviews.

Erskine, Hazel. 1973. "The Polls: Hopes, Fears, and Regrets." Public Opinion Quarterly 37:132-45.

Eyde, Lorraine D. 1968. "Work Motivation of Women College Graduates: Five-Year Follow-up." Journal of Counseling Psychology 15 (March):199-202.

Fabe, Marilyn, and Norma Wikler. 1979. Up Against the Clock: Career Women Speak on the Choice to Have Children. New York: Random House.

Faver, Catherine A. 1982a. "Achievement Orientation, Attainment Values, and Women's Employment." Journal of Vocational Behavior 20 (February):67-80.

____. 1982b. "Life Satisfaction and the Life-Cycle: The Effects of Values and Roles on Women's Well-Being." Sociology and Social Research 66 (July):435-51.

___. 1981. "Women, Careers, and Family: Generational and Life-Cycle Effects on Achievement Orientation." Journal of Family Issues 2 (March):91-112.

___. 1979. "Women and Achievement Orientation Across the Life-Cycle." Ph.D. dissertation, University of Michigan. Dissertation Abstracts International 40:2924-A.

Feldman, Saul D. 1973. "Impediment or Stimulant? Marital Status and Graduate Education." In Changing Women in a Changing Society, pp. 220-32. Edited by Joan Huber. Chicago: University of Chicago Press.

Fox, Mary Frank, and Catherine A. Faver. 1981. "Achievement and Aspiration: Patterns Among Male and Female Academic-Career Aspirants." Sociology of Work and Occupations 8 (November):439-63.

Fox, Mary Frank, and Sharlene Hesse-Biber. 1984. Women at Work. Palo Alto, Calif.: Mayfield Publishing Co.

French, Elizabeth G., and Gerald S. Lesser. 1964. "Some Characteristics of the Achievement Motive in Women." Journal of Abnormal and Social Psychology 68 (February):119-28.

Friedan, Betty. 1963. The Feminine Mystique. New York: Norton.

Glenn, Norval D. 1975. "Psychological Well-being in the Postparental Stage: Some Evidence from National Surveys." Journal of Marriage and the Family 37:105-10.

Gluck, Nora R., Elaine Dannefer, and Kathryn Milea. 1980. "Women in Families." In The Family Life Cycle: A Framework for Family Therapy, pp. 295-327. Edited by Elizabeth A. Carter and Monica McGoldrick. New York: Gardner Press.

Gould, J.A., and A. Pagano. 1972. "Sex Discrimination and Achievement." National Association of Women Deans and Counselors Journal (Winter):74-82.

Gove, Walter R., and Jeannette F. Tudor. 1973. "Adult Sex Roles and Mental Illness." In Changing Women in a Changing Society, pp. 50-73. Edited by Joan Huber. Chicago: University of Chicago Press.

Greenwald, C. S. 1977. "Part-Time Work." In American Women Workers in a Full Employment Economy, pp. 182-91. Washington, D.C.: U.S. Government Printing Office.

Hacker, A. 1979. "Divorce a la Mode." New York Review of Books (26 May):23-27.

Harkins, Elizabeth B. 1978. "Effects of the Empty Nest Transition: A Self Report of Psychological Well Being." Journal of Marriage and the Family 40 (August):549-56.

Harmon, Lenore W. 1970. "Anatomy of Career Commitment in Women." Journal of Counseling Psychology 17, no. 1:77-80.

Harmon, Lenore W. 1967. "Women's Working Patterns Related to Their SVIB Housewife and 'Own' Occupational Scores." Journal of Counseling Psychology 14:299-301.

Hauserman, Nancy R. 1980. "The American Homemaker: Policy Proposals." In Women's Lives: New Theory, Research & Policy, pp. 397-403. Edited by Dorothy G. McGuigan. Ann Arbor: University of Michigan Center for Continuing Education of Women.

Havens, Elizabeth M. 1973. "Women, Work, and Wedlock: A Note on Female Marital Patterns in the United States." In Changing Women in a Changing Society, pp. 213-19. Edited by Joan Huber. Chicago: University of Chicago Press.

Helson, Ravenna. 1975. "The Changing Image of the Career Woman." In Women and Achievement: Social and Motivational Analyses, pp. 420-31. Edited by Martha T. S. Mednick, Sandra S. Tangri, and Lois W. Hoffman. Washington, D.C.: Hemisphere Publishing.

Herman, Sonya J. 1977. "Women, Divorce, and Suicide." Journal of Divorce 1 (Winter):107-17.

Hesselbart, Susan. 1980. "An Evaluation of Sex Role Theories: The Clash Between Idealism and Reality." Paper presented at the annual meetings of the Association for Consumer Research, Arlington, Va., October.

___. 1978. "Some Underemphasized Issues About Men, Women, and Work." Paper presented at the annual meetings of the American Sociological Association, San Francisco, August.

Hill, Reuben, and Roy H. Rodgers. 1964. "The Developmental Approach." In Handbook of Marriage and the Family, pp. 171-211. Edited by Harold T. Christensen. Chicago: Rand McNally.

Hofferth, Sandra L., and Kristin A. Moore. 1979. "Women's Employment and Marriage." In The Subtle Revolution, pp. 99-124. Edited by R. E. Smith. Washington, D.C.: The Urban Institute.

Hoffman, Lois W. 1979. "Maternal Employment: 1979." American Psychologist 34:859-65.

___. 1975. "Early Childhood Experiences and Women's Achievement Motives." In Women and Achievement: Social and Motivational Analyses, pp. 129-50. Edited by Martha T. S. Mednick, Sandra S. Tangri, and Lois W. Hoffman. Washington, D.C.: Hemisphere Publishing.

Horner, Matina S. 1972. "Toward An Understanding of Achievement-Related Conflicts in Women." Journal of Social Issues 28 (Spring):157-75.

Houseknecht, Sharon K. 1979. "Childlessness and Marital Adjustment." Journal of Marriage and the Family 41, no. 2 (May):259-65.

Hunt, Morton. 1966. The World of the Formerly Married. New York: McGraw-Hill.

Huston-Stein, Aletha, and Ann Higgins-Trenk. 1978. "Development of Females from Childhood Through Adulthood: Career and Feminine Role Orientations." In Life Span Development and Behavior. Vol. I, pp. 257-96. Edited by Paul B. Baltes. New York: Academic Press.

Kagan, Jerome, and Howard A. Moss. 1962. Birth to Maturity: A Study in Psychological Development. New York: Wiley.

Kamerman, Sheila B., and Alfred J. Kahn. 1981. Child Care, Family Benefits, and Working Parents: A Study in Comparative Policy. New York: Columbia University Press.

Kanter, Rosabeth M. 1977. Men and Women of the Corporation. New York: Basic Books.

Kaufman, Debra R., and Barbara L. Richardson. 1982. Achievement and Women: Challenging the Assumptions. New York: The Free Press.

Komarovsky, Mirra. 1973. "Cultural Contradictions and Sex Roles: The Masculine Case." In Changing Women in a Changing Society, pp. 111-22. Edited by Joan Huber. Chicago: University of Chicago Press.

Kreps, Juanita M., and R. John Leaper. 1976. "Home Work, Market Work, and the Allocation of Time." In Women and the American Economy: A Look to the 1980s, pp. 61-81. Edited by Juanita M. Kreps. Englewood Cliffs, N.J.: Prentice-Hall.

Land, Hilary. 1980. "Social Policies and the Family: Their Effect on Women's Employment in Great Britain." In Equal Employment Policy for Women, pp. 366-88. Edited by R. S. Ratner. Philadelphia: Temple University Press.

Laws, Judith Long. 1978. "Work Motivation and Work Behavior of Women: New Perspectives." In The Psychology of Women: Future Directions in Research, pp. 285-348. Edited by Julia A. Sherman and Florence L. Denmark. New York: Psychological Dimensions.

Lenhoff, Donna. 1980. "Equal Pay for Work of Comparable Value as Strategy." In Manual on Pay Equity, pp. 57-58. Edited by J. Grune. Washington, D.C.: Conference on Alternative State and Local Policies.

Lesser, Gerald S. 1973. "Achievement Motivation in Women." In Human Motivation: A Book of Readings, pp. 202-21. Edited by David C. McClelland and Robert S. Steele. Morristown, N.J.: General Learning Press.

Levinson, Daniel J., Charlotte N. Darrow, Edward B. Klein, Maria H. Levinson, and Braxton McKee. 1978. The Seasons of a Man's Life. New York: Ballantine Books.

Lipman-Blumen, Jean, and Harold J. Leavitt. 1977. "Vicarious and Direct Achievement Patterns in Adulthood." In Counseling Adults, pp. 60-76. Edited by Nancy K. Schlossberg and Alan D. Entine. Monterey, Calif.: Brooks/Cole.

Lloyd, Cynthia B., and Beth T. Niemi. 1979. The Economics of Sex Differentials. New York: Columbia University Press.

Long, Larry H. 1974. "Women's Labor Force Participation and Residential Mobility." Social Forces 52, no. 3 (March):342-48.

Lopata, Helena Znaniecka. 1979. Women as Widows. New York: Elsevier.

Lopata, Helena, and F. Steinhart. 1971. "Work Histories of American Urban Women." Gerontologist 2, no. 4:27-28.

Lowenthal, Marjorie F. 1975. "Psychosocial Variations Across the Adult Life Course: Frontiers for Research and Policy." The Gerontologist 15:6-12.

McClelland, David C., John W. Atkinson, A. Russell Clark, and Edgar L. Lowell. 1953. The Achievement Motive. New York: Appleton-Century Crofts.

McGuigan, Dorothy G., ed. 1978. The University of Michigan Center for Continuing Education of Women, 1964-1977: A Report. Ann Arbor: University of Michigan Center for Continuing Education of Women.

Manis, Jean D., and Hazel Markus. 1978. "Careers and Career Attitudes: Age, Education, and Timing Effects." Paper presented at the annual meeting of the American Psychological Association, Toronto, 30 August.

Meile, Richard L., David R. Johnson, and Louis St. Peter. 1976. "Marital Role, Education, and Mental Disorder Among Women: Test of an Interaction Hypothesis." Journal of Health and Social Behavior 17:295-301.

Meissner, Martin, Elizabeth Humphreys, Scott Meiss, and William J. Scheu. 1975. "No Exit for Wives: Sexual Division of Labour and the Cumulation of Household Demands." Canadian Review of Sociology and Anthropology 12:424-39.

Mikus, Karen C. 1980. "Psychological Correlates of Early Family Formation." In Women's Lives: New Theory, Research & Policy, pp. 117-26. Edited by Dorothy G. McGuigan. Ann Arbor: University of Michigan Center for Continuing Education of Women.

Miller, Ann R. 1966. "Migration Differentials in Labor Force Participation: United States, 1960." Demography 3, no. 1:58-67.

Moore, Kristin A., and Isabel V. Sawhill. 1976. "Implications of Women's Employment for Home and Family Life." In Women and the American Economy: A Look to the 1980s, pp. 102-22. Edited by Juanita M. Kreps. Englewood Cliffs, N.J.: Prentice-Hall.

Mulvey, Mary C. 1963. "Psychological and Sociological Factors in Prediction of Career Patterns of Women." Genetic Psychology Monographs 68:309-86.

Bernice L. Neugarten. 1979. "Time, Age, and the Life Cycle." American Journal of Psychiatry 136:887-94.

____. 1977. "Adaptation and the Life-Cycle." In Counseling Adults, pp. 34-46. Edited by Nancy K. Schlossberg and Alan D. Entine. Monterey, Calif.: Brooks/Cole.

Nye, F. Ivan. 1974. "Effects on Mother." In Working Mothers, pp. 207-25. Edited by Lois W. Hoffman and F. Ivan Nye. San Francisco: Jossey-Bass.

Parelius, Ann P. 1975. "Change and Stability in College Women's Orientations Toward Education, Family, and Work." Social Problems 22, no. 3 (February):420-32.

Parsons, Jacquelynne E., and Susan B. Goff. 1978. "Achievement Motivation and Values: An Alternative Perspective." Michigan Occasional Paper no. 3 (Fall).

Pleck, Joseph H. 1981. "The Work-Family Problem: Overloading the System." In Outsiders on the Inside: Women and Organizations, pp. 239-54. Edited by B. L. Forisha and B. H. Goldman. Englewood Cliffs, N.J.: Prentice-Hall.

Plunkett, Marcia W. 1980. "Meanings of Work for Mothers." In Women's Lives: New Theory, Research & Policy, pp. 95-99. Edited by Dorothy G. McGuigan. Ann Arbor: University of Michigan Center for Continuing Education of Women.

Poloma, Margaret M. 1972. "Role Conflict and the Married Professional Woman." In Toward a Sociology of Women, pp. 187-99. Edited by Constantina Safilios-Rothschild. Lexington, Mass.: Xerox College Publishing.

Powell, Barbara. 1977. "The Empty Nest, Employment, and Psychiatric Symptoms in College-Educated Women." Psychology of Women Quarterly 2, no. 1 (Fall):35-43.

Radloff, Lenore. 1975. "Sex Differences in Depression: The Effects of Occupation and Marital Status." Sex Roles 1:249-65.

Ratner, Ronnie S. 1980. Equal Employment Policy for Women. Philadelphia: Temple University Press.

Rossi, Alice S. 1980. "Life-Span Theories and Women's Lives." Signs: Journal of Women in Culture and Society 6 (Autumn):4-32.

____. 1968. "Transition to Parenthood." Journal of Marriage and the Family 30 (February):26-39.

____. 1966. "The Roots of Ambivalence in American Women." Revision of a paper presented to the Adult Education Association, Chicago. 15 November.

Safilios-Rothschild, Constantina. 1974. Women and Social Policy. Englewood Cliffs, N.J.: Prentice-Hall.

Scarf, Maggie. 1980. Unfinished Business: Pressure Points in the Lives of Women. Garden City, N.Y.: Doubleday.

Schaie, K. W. 1970. "A Reinterpretation of Age-Related Changes in Cognitive Structure and Functioning." In Life-Span Developmental Psychology, pp. 485-507. Edited by L. R. Goulet and P. B. Baltes. New York: Academic Press.

Schwartz, Pamela M. 1980. "Working Mothers of Infants: Conflicts and Coping Strategies." In Women's Lives: New Theory, Research & Policy, pp. 85-94. Edited by Dorothy G. McGuigan. Ann Arbor: University of Michigan Center for Continuing Education of Women.

Sears, Pauline S., and Ann H. Barbee. 1977. "Career and Life Satisfaction Among Terman's Gifted Women." In The Gifted and the Creative: Fifty-Year Perspective, pp. 28-65. Edited by J. Stanley, W. George, and C. Solano. Baltimore: Johns Hopkins University Press.

Sheehy, Gail. 1974. Passages: Predictable Crises of Adult Life. New York: Dutton.

Smith, M.B. 1969. Social Psychology and Human Values. Chicago: Aldine.

Smith, Ralph E. 1979. "The Movement of Women into the Labor Market." In The Subtle Revolution: Women at Work, pp. 1-29. Edited by Ralph E. Smith. Washington, D.C.: The Urban Institute.

___. 1978. "The Effects of Hours Rigidity on the Labor Force Status of Women." The Urban and Social Change Review 11:43-47.

Sontag, Susan. 1975. "The Double Standard of Aging." In No Longer Young: The Older Woman in America, pp. 31-39. Ann Arbor/Detroit: University of Michigan/Wayne State University, Institute of Gerontology.

Spreitzer, Elmer, Eldon E. Snyder, and David Larson. 1975. "Age, Marital Status, and Labor Force Participation as Related to Life Satisfaction." Sex Roles 1:235-47.

Stein, Aletha H., and Margaret M. Bailey. 1976. "The Socialization of Achievement Orientation in Females." In Beyond Sex-Role Stereotypes: Readings Toward a Psychology of Androgyny, pp. 240-61. Edited by Alexandra G. Kaplan and Joan P. Bean. Boston: Little, Brown and Co.

Stein, Aletha H., Sheila R. Pohly, and Edward Mueller. 1971. "The Influence of Masculine, Feminine, and Neutral Tasks on Children's Achievement Behavior, Expectancies of Success, and Attainment Values." Child Development 42 (March):195-207.

Sweet, James A. 1973. Women in the Labor Force. New York: Seminar Press.

Taeuber, Karl E., and James A. Sweet. 1976. "Family and Work: The Social Life Cycle of Women." In Women and the American Economy: A Look to the 1980s, pp. 31-60. Edited by Juanita M. Kreps. Englewood Cliffs, N.J.: Prentice-Hall.

Tangri, Sandra S. 1975. "Implied Demand Character of the Wife's Future and Role Innovation: Patterns of Achievement Orientation Among College Women." In Women and Achievement: Social and Motivational Analyses, pp. 239-54. Edited by Martha T. S. Mednick, Sandra S. Tangri, and Lois W. Hoffman. Washington, D.C.: Hemisphere Publishing.

___. "Determinants of Occupational Role Innovation Among College Women." Journal of Social Issues 28 (Spring):177-99.

Tcheng-Laroche, Francoise, and Raymond H. Prince. 1979. "Middle Income, Divorced Female Heads of Families: Their Lifestyles, Health and Stress Levels." Canadian Journal of Psychiatry 24:35-42.

Troll, Lillian E. 1975. Early and Middle Adulthood: The Best Is Yet to Be--Maybe. Monterey, Calif.: Brooks/Cole, Wadsworth.

Troll, Lillian E., Bernice L. Neugarten, and R. J. Kraines. 1969. "Similarities in Values and Other Personality Characteristics in College Students and Their Parents." Merrill-Palmer Quarterly 15 (October):323-37.

U.S. Department of Commerce, Bureau of the Census. 1980. A Statistical Portrait of Women in the United States: 1978. Current Population Reports, Special Studies, Series P-23, no. 100. Washington, D.C.: U.S. Government Printing Office.

___. 1978. Statistical Abstract of the United States: 1978. 99th ed. Washington, D.C.: U.S. Government Printing Office.

___. 1977. "Fertility of American Women: June 1976." Current Population Reports, Series P-20, no. 308. Washington, D.C.: U.S. Government Printing Office.

U.S. Department of Labor, Women's Bureau. 1975. 1975 Handbook on Women Workers. Bulletin no. 297. Washington, D.C.: U.S. Government Printing Office.

___. 1966. College Women Seven Years After Graduation: Resurvey of Women Graduates--Class of 1957. Bulletin no. 292. Reported by Jean A. Wells. Washington, D.C.: U.S. Government Printing Office.

University of Michigan, Statistical Research Laboratory. 1976. Elementary Statistics Using Midas. 2nd ed. Ann Arbor: University of Michigan Press.

Van Dusen, Roxann A., and Eleanor B. Sheldon. 1976. "The Changing Status of American Women: A Life Cycle Perspective." American Psychologist 31, no. 2 (February):106-16.

Veroff, Joseph. 1969. "Social Comparison and the Development of Achievement Motivation." In Achievement-Related Motives in Children, pp. 46-101. Edited by Charles P. Smith. New York: Russell Sage.

Veroff, Joseph, and Sheila Feld. 1970. Marriage and Work in America. New York: Van Nostrand Reinhold.

Veroff, Joseph, Lou McClelland, and Kent Marquis. 1971. "Measuring Intelligence and Achievement Motivation in Surveys." Final Report to the U.S. Department of Health, Education and Welfare, Office of Economic Opportunity, Contract no. OEO-4180. Ann Arbor: Survey Research Center, Institute for Social Research, University of Michigan.

Veroff, Joseph, Lou McClelland, and David Ruhland. 1975. "Varieties of Achievement Motivation." In Women and Achievement: Social and Motivational Analyses, pp. 172-205. Edited by Martha T. S. Mednick, Sandra S. Tangri, and Lois W. Hoffman. Washington, D.C.: Hemisphere Publishing.

Voydanoff, Patricia. 1980. "Work-Family Life Cycle Among Women." In Women's Lives: New Theory, Research & Policy, pp. 61-8. Edited by Dorothy G. McGuigan. Ann Arbor: University of Michigan Center for Continuing Education of Women.

Weiss, Robert S. and Nancy Samelson. 1958. "Social Roles of American Women: Their Contribution to a Sense of Usefulness and Importance." Marriage and Family Living 20 (November):358-66.

Yankelovich, Daniel. 1981. New Rules: Searching for Fulfillment in a World Turned Upside Down. New York: Random House.

Zeitlin, Maurice. 1967. Revolutionary Politics and the Cuban Working Class. Princeton, N.J.: Princeton University Press.

Zellman, Gail L. 1976. "The Role of Structural Factors in Limiting Women's Institutional Participation." Journal of Social Issues 32 (Summer):33-46.

INDEX

achievement orientation: age cohort comparison, 37, 41-44, 138; for ages 22-34, 59-60; for ages 35-44, 94-96; for ages 45-64, 118-19; career orientation and, 14, 15, 19, 20, 21, 22; employment status and, 16-18, 19, 21, 22, 23, 41-44, 138; family values and, 19-23; life-cycle stage and, 15-17, 18, 41-42, 60, 94, 96, 112, 138; scaled in the study group, 32; stability in, 15-18, 37, 138, 140; theory and research, 9-15; variations in the expression of, 19-23

adult development, 2-9

affiliation: achievement orientation and, 11, 12, 13, 18; married, childless women and, 57

affirmative action, 145

age cohorts, 6, 7, 8, 29, 30, 35-37; achievement orientation among, 37, 41-44, 138; career orientation among, 36, 39, 41,-42, 43, 120, 138; career values among, 39-42, 43, 44-47, 120-121, 138-39; defined, 3; employment status among, 42-47, 126, 139; family values among, 39-41, 44-47, 99, 138-39; life satisfaction among, 47-52, 139. See also ages 22-34; ages 35-44; ages 45-64; generations

"agentic achievement," 13

ages 22-34, 30, 55-89; achievement orientation, 59-60; career orientation, 62-65, 72-77, 109; career values, 46, 58-59, 66-70, 72-77, 110; employment status, 46, 57, 58, 59, 70-77, 87-88, 102, 110, 111; family values, 46, 66-70, 75, 110, 111; life satisfaction, 77-88

ages 35-44, 30, 35, 91-112; achievement orientation, 94-96; career orientation, 63-64, 96-97, 103-4, 109; career values, 46, 97-100, 103-4, 105, 107, 110; employment status, 46, 100-4, 105, 107, 110, 111; family values, 46, 99-100, 107, 110, 111; life satisfaction, 104-7

ages 45-64, 30, 35, 113-36; achievement orientation, 118-19; career orientation, 120, 126-27; career values, 46, 120-23, 126-27; employment status, 46, 125-27; family values, 120-23, 130; life satisfaction, 128-35

ABOUT THE AUTHOR

CATHERINE ANN FAVER is an associate professor in social work at the University of Tennessee, Knoxville. Until 1983 she was an assistant professor in social work at the University of Texas at Arlington.

Dr. Faver has published in the areas of both sociology and social work. Her articles have appeared in Journal of Family Issues, Sociology and Social Research, Journal of Vocational Behavior, and Journal of Education for Social Work.

Dr. Faver holds a B.A. from Hardin-Simmons University, an M.S.S.W. from the University of Texas at Arlington, and an M.A. and Ph.D. from the University of Michigan.